PAGE CYCLE DIET COOKBOOK

PAGE CYCLE DIET COOKBOOK

MIKE PAGE
JENNIFER DU CHARME

PAGE CYCLE, LLC

SALT LAKE CITY, UTAH

Disclaimer: This publication contains the opinions and ideas of its author. It is intended to provide helpful and informative material on subjects addressed in the publication. It is sold with the understanding that the author is not engaged in rendering medical, health, or any other kind of personal professional services in the book. The reader should consult his or her medical, health, or any other competent professional before adopting any of the suggestions in this book or drawing inferences from it.
The author specifically disclaims all responsibility for any liability, loss, or risk, personal or otherwise, which is incurred as a consequence, directly or indirectly, of the use and application of any of the contents of this book. References are provided for informational purposes only and do not constitute endorsement of any websites or other sources. Readers should be aware that the websites listed in this book may change.

Page Cycle Diet Cookbook
Page, Mike &
Du Charme, Jennifer
Published by: Page Cycle, LLC., Salt Lake City, Utah

First Edition, Published 2012

Printed in the United States of America

Editor and Interior Design & Layout: Jennifer Du Charme
Cover Art Design: Jennifer R. Phillips, JRP Design
Copy Editor: Talya Drissman

ISBN-13: 978-1478103776
ISBN-10: 1478103779

To all the Page Cycle Fans loosing weight and learning new lifestyle and way of cooking. Thank you for taking control of your life and your body!

CONTENTS

1

Food is...

Food is….. Essential to human life, entertainment, ritual, celebration, family, holidays, happiness, enjoyable, amazing, fulfilling, beautiful, aromatic, sensational, art, medicine, poison, healing, addictive, mental, physical, power, weakness, satisfaction, nutrition, creation, sweet, salty, sour, strong, weak, hot, cold, FUEL!!!

And if you're like me, you have a LOVE/HATE relationship with food that, most of the time, is frustrating and confusing! Let me explain… For most of my adult life, I was miserable when I ate the foods I loved because I didn't look the way I wanted. And I was miserable when I gave up the foods I loved to look the way I wanted! I lived like this for close to 25 years…

Until I developed the Page Cycle Diet and found a way I could still eat the foods I love and look the way I wanted all at the same time. I can't articulate the significant impact this had on my life. I no longer had to feel torn between looking good and eating the foods I love. In November 2011, I published the Page Cycle Diet as a gift to all of those people that have the same or similar relationship to food that I used to have.

The Purpose of this Cookbook is to give you a tool that will teach you how to prepare food that you love and empower you to look the way you want…

My Goal is for this book to change your life and impact you in a very profound way!!!

Before you get into the recipes, I want to explain two concepts that are critical for you to understand if you're going to have long term success on the Page Cycle Diet. I wish these two concepts were black & white. It would make my job as your coach a lot easier and would certainly make your job as a student so much simpler.

My goal is to empower you and to do that, I can't take the easy road and neither can you…

Concept # 1

Incidental Carbs – The easiest way for me to explain this is to use a couple of examples:

Cottage Cheese
Serving size: 1 cup 2% low fat
Calories: 194
Fat: 6 grams
Protein: 27 grams
Carbs: 8 grams

As you can see, cottage cheese is primarily made up of protein and fat, but it does contain 8 grams of carbohydrates. The best way for me to explain is that the "essence" of cottage cheese is protein and fat, not carbohydrates.

Oatmeal
Serving size: ½ cup
Calories: 150
Fat: 3 g

Protein: 5 g
Carbohydrates: 27 g

Oatmeal contains protein and fat but its "ESSENCE" is carbohydrates. I know what most of you are thinking, "is there a ratio or a number that determines what the essence of a recipe or a dish is?" The answer is no, there isn't an exact number. In general, if a product comes from an animal (not something that is grown), the essence is a protein or healthy fat. Likewise, if something is grown, its essence is a carbohydrate.

So - as you look at the chart in the back of the book, you will see that they are marked with an 'x' to determine which cycle in which they can be used. You will notice that some of them contain "Incidental carbohydrates," but, in most cases, the amount of carbohydrates in them is so minimal that they are considered incidental. As such, that recipe will be okay on all protein days. Again, some of these recipes aren't black and white, which makes it a judgment call on my part.

The other thing I want you to understand is that you can make almost all the recipes suitable for the Extreme Burn Cycle if you simply don't eat the carbohydrates in the recipe. Many times I will make a recipe with the carbohydrates but will eat around the carbs. That way, I still get the taste of adding onions or other flavorful vegetables without actually eating them.

Concept # 2

With all the billions of people in the world, no two people have the same DNA or fingerprints. As a coach I have to give the best advice I can to the largest percentage of people. I'm telling you this because I need you to play an active role in your own path through this process.

I need you to pay attention and learn how your body responds to the Page Cycle Diet and its different cycles. I pay close attention to my body and usually when my body fat starts creeping up it's because I'm either not eating enough carbohydrates or I allow too much sugar into my diet.

I don't write things down, but I do consciously pay attention to my diet. This allows me to make corrections to get the results I'm looking for. I encourage you to get to know your body and how it responds in order for you to be in complete control of your results.

You may be a person that needs to have very few carbs in order to get the results you want or you may need more carbs than what I have outlined. Either way, no one knows your body like you do and if you don't know it well enough, then now is the time to got to know yourself.

Mike Page, Body Challenge Coach

2

Page Cycle Diet Cooking Basics

Cooking on The Page Cycle diet is easy. I know that once you get the hang of it you will be able to come up with your own recipes of foods that you love and maybe even learn some new ones. When you are cooking on the Plan it can be something as easy as a grilled chicken breast for dinner with some steamed broccoli. However, I know that, for some people, that may become tedious. That is where the Cookbook comes in. In here, there are some more complex recipes, full of flavor, that will keep you from getting bored with your food.

The key to making this work with The Page Cycle Diet is planning. I cannot stress this enough. In fact, I know I told you this in The Page Cycle Diet Book, but I am telling you this again. The biggest failure comes from when people let themselves get too hungry and then… anything will do. They reach for the first thing they find and it may not always be what they should be eating. So, in the back of the book, you will find menu planners. Please use them as a 'getting started guide' of sorts but feel free to swap out foods for other recipes that better fit your taste and time. Cooking foods to have extra servings (which will leave you leftovers) is another good way to keep good foods on hand in case you are hungry and don't have time to cook something.

When you are cooking with the Page Cycle Diet and looking to cut out the carbs, always keep an eye on the sugar. There are many great sugar substitutes out there and anything listed can be swapped it with your favorite. I recommend always having a sugar substitute on hand as a new pantry basic.

Another great staple that can be easily substituted into many of current recipes is almond flour. Almond flour is just that: flour made from ground up almonds. It will provide a similar consistency to flour, imparts a mild taste, and will give you the texture you are looking for. In addition to almond flour, you may also use soy flour.

Instead of using bread crumbs in a recipe, try crushed pork rinds. They will simulate the crunchyness of bread crumbs and supply the starch-like texture but with no carbs.

The last two are probably my favorites and my most commonly used. Swap out lettuce leaves for any bread in a sandwich. I make lettuce wraps out of everything! I will even use it in place of tortillas in my tacos. The other one is so useful and can be done at anytime on the Page Cycle Diet - even during Extreme Burn - and that is using celery in place of crackers or chips for all dip recipes.

Keep in mind that you can learn a new way of living and still have fun on the weekends. I know that, with time, these simple swaps will become a new way of cooking for you. They will have you cooking up a storm and enjoying food with a new comfort level.

3

Breakfast

Protein Pancakes - Jen's Way

High Protein, Low Carb Pancakes.

20 Minutes to Prepare and Cook

Ingredients

1 Whole Egg
1/4 Cup. Fat Free Cottage Cheese
1/4 Cup. Old Fashioned Oatmeal (powdered in blender)
2 Scoops
1/8 teaspoon Maple Extract
Water

Directions

Blend all ingredients together in a blender until it forms a batter-like consistency.

Spray a non-stick skillet with cooking spray & cook batter into 3 pancakes.

Makes 3 Pancakes or 1 serving.

Crustless Spinach Mini Quiches

These are great because the leftovers make an easy breakfast that you can warm up a couple of these in the microwave and run.

Ingredients

1 tablespoon vegetable oil
1 onion, chopped
1 (10 ounce) package frozen chopped spinach, thawed and drained
5 eggs, beaten
3 cups shredded Muenster cheese
1/4 teaspoon salt
1/8 teaspoon ground black pepper

Directions

Preheat oven to 350 degrees F (175 degrees Cup). Lightly spray a muffin pan with nonstick cooking spray.

Heat oil in a large skillet over medium-high heat. Add onions and cook, stirring occasionally, until onions are soft. Stir in spinach and continue cooking until excess moisture has evaporated.

In a large bowl, combine eggs, cheese, salt and pepper. Add spinach mixture and stir to blend. Scoop into prepared pie pan.

Bake in preheated oven until eggs have set, about 20 minutes. Let cool for 10 minutes before serving.

Smoked Salmon Scramble

Ingredients

6 eggs
1 1/2 tablespoons butter
Salt
Freshly ground black pepper
4 ounces smoked salmon, cut into 1/2-inch dice
4 ounces cream cheese, cut into 1/2-inch dice
Minced chives for garnish

Directions

Put the eggs, butter, and some salt and pepper in a skillet. Heat to medium-high and begin to beat the mixture with a whisk, stirring almost constantly but not too fast; you do not want the mixture to become foamy.

Once the butter has melted, the mixture will begin to thicken and develop small curds; this will take from 3 to 8 minutes. If the eggs begin to stick to the bottom of the pan, remove from the heat for a moment, continuing to whisk, and then return to the flame.

When the eggs are very creamy, with small curds all over--not unlike very loose oatmeal--they are just about ready. Stir in the smoked salmon and cook for a minute, just to warm it. Remove from the heat, stir in the cream cheese and taste for salt and pepper. Garnish with chives.

Caramel Latte Blended Ice Coffee Shake

My favorite weekday breakfast when I need some get up and go! I have forgotten all about that other place, what was it called, four-bucks?

Ingredients

8 oz ice cold milk
1 tablespoon Instant Espresso Powder
2 Scoops Sweet Cream Protein Powder
1 teaspoon Sugar Free Caramel Syrup (Torani)
1/2 cup of Ice

Directions

Pour all the ingredients into a blender mix and enjoy!

Breakfast Pudding

Ingredients

1/3 cup ricotta cheese
1 egg
3 tablespoons half and half
1 tablespoon flax seed meal
Vanilla sugar-free syrup to taste
1 pinch cinnamon

Directions

Mix cheese, egg and half and half together in a saucepan - cook stirring over medium heat until thick.

Add flax and syrup.

Sprinkle with cinnamon.

Makes enough for two servings.

Cinnamon Muffins

Ingredients

3 eggs
1/4 cup plus 2 tablespoons oil
1/4 cup sugar free syrup, such as Da Vinci
2 tablespoons water
1 tablespoon vanilla
1 cup flax meal
1/2 teaspoon baking soda
1/2 teaspoon baking powder
2 tablespoons cinnamon

Directions

In a medium bowl, beat the eggs with a fork. With a fork or spoon, beat in oil, syrup, water and vanilla.

In small bowl, combine remaining dry ingredients, then stir into egg mixture. Let stand 5 minutes.

Spoon into 12 well-greased muffin cups (without papers).

Bake at 350° F 12-15 minutes, or until they are lightly browned and seem set to the touch. Remove from tin at once to cooling rack.

Store in refrigerator.

Makes 12 muffins

Mock Oatmeal

Wonderful texture (mouth feel) and taste PLUS protein and lots of fiber!

Ingredients

2 tablespoons flax seed meal
2 tablespoons textured soy protein
1/2 cup water
1 packet Splenda
2 dashes cinnamon
1 tablespoon half and half

Directions

Combine flax meal and tvp with water and microwave for 1 to 1.5 minutes on high.

Stir in Splenda to taste, a few shakes of cinnamon and pour on the cream.

On The Go Breakfast Cookies

Quick high protein high fiber breakfast/snack

17 Minutes to Prepare and Cook

Ingredients

16 tablespoon. Flax Seed Meal (ground flax)
8 teaspoon. Splenda Brown Sugar Blend
1 cup Peanut Butter, chunk style
1 teaspoon Baking Soda
2 large Eggs, fresh

Directions

Preheat oven to 350° F .

Mix flax and baking soda together, then add egg mix with peanut butter until creamy.

Teaspoon onto and bake on a no-stick baking pan for 12 minutes.

Makes 12 servings. 2 cookies per serving.

Baked Egg Muffins

Great Extreme Burn Recipe that's easy to make for a large groups or can be made ahead of time and warmed up during the week.

15-20 Minutes to Prep and Cook

Ingredients

6 oz Turkey or Ham
3/4 Cup Salsa (Garden Fresh Gourmet Brand)
2 1/4 Cups of Liquid Egg Whites (May use Egg Beaters or Scrambled Eggs)
2 tablespoon grated low fat Cheddar Cheese

Directions

Preheat oven to 400° F .

Spray muffin pan with nonstick cooking spray.

Line each muffin cup in the pan with about 1/4 oz of Turkey.

Spoon about a tablespoon of salsa on top of the turkey.

Add 3 tablespoons of Eggs into each muffin cup

Bake the tray for 10-12 minutes or until eggs are no longer runny.

Remove from oven and top with cheese.

Makes 6 servings.

Cinnamon Rolls

Ingredients:

3 eggs, separated
3 oz Cream Cheese, room temperature
Dash Salt
1 drop liquid Splenda or liquid equivalent
1 teaspoon Cinnamon
1/2 teaspoon Cream of Tartar
-Icing-
4 oz Cream Cheese
4 tablespoon Butter
4 packets of truvia or splenda (pulsed in coffee grinder or magic bullet cup)
4 drops of liquid splenda
1/2 teaspoon Lemon juice
1/2 teaspoon Vanilla
1/2 teaspoon Cinnamon
1 tablespoon Heavy Cream
2 tablespoon Water

Directions

Preheat oven to 300°F. Spray Pam on a nonstick or parchment lined cookie sheet.

Separate eggs very carefully (make sure that none of the yolk gets into the whites.) In the bowl of an electric mixer place the egg whites with cream of tartar and beat on medium/medium high until whites are stiff but not dry.

In a separate bowl mix together yolks, cottage cheese, Splenda, Cinnamon and a dash of salt. Beat together until the yolks and the cream cheese are mixed smoothly.

Fold together the egg whites with the yolk mixture. Be very careful not to break down the egg whites. Mix for no more than 1 minute.

Place the mixture carefully on the non stick cookie sheet, gently putting one tablespoon full on top of another until each "roll" is about 2 inches high. Repeat this until you have 6 piles.

Place the cookie sheet in the oven and bake for about 30 minutes.

While the rolls are baking, in the bowl of an electric mixer place the cream cheese and butter. Mix together until creamy and mixed. Scrape down the sides of the mixer.

Add in the powdered truvia, liquid splenda, Lemon juice, and Vanilla, and mix together. Then add the Cream and Water and mix again. Lastly add in the cinnamon and blend one final time. Place the icing into the fridge for 20 minutes.

While the rolls are warm after removing from the oven top with the icing and enjoy!

Makes 6-8 servings.

Chocolate Donuts with Peanut Butter Glaze

Ingredients

1 1/4 cups peanut flour
1/3 cup cocoa powder
1/4 cup granulated erythritol
1 teaspoon baking powder
1/4 teaspoon baking soda
1/2 teaspoon salt
2 large eggs, lightly beaten
2 tablespoons coconut oil, melted
1/2 teaspoon vanilla extract
8 drops stevia extract
1/4 cup almond milk
GLAZE:
2 tablespoons peanut butter
2 tablespoons whipping cream
2 tablespoons almond milk
1 tablespoon powdered erythritol
6 drops stevia extract
2 tablespoons peanuts, chopped (for garnish)

Directions

Preheat oven to 325 degrees F and grease a donut tin.

In a large bowl whisk together peanut flour, cocoa powder, granulated erythritol, baking powder, baking soda, and salt. In another small bowl, whisk together eggs, coconut oil, vanilla and stevia. Add egg mixture to peanut flour mixture and stir until thoroughly combined. Add almond milk and stir until smooth.

Fill holes of donut tin 2/3 full (you will likely have to do 2 batches). Bake for 18 to 20 minutes, or until set and donuts spring back when touched. Let cool in pan 5 minutes and then flip out onto a wire rack to cool completely. Repeat with remaining batter.

For the glaze, place peanut butter in a microwave-safe dish, and warm gently in 20 second intervals until peanut butter is very soft. Stir in whipping cream and almond milk until smooth and well combined. Stir in powdered erythritol and stevia. Spread glaze onto donuts with a knife. The glaze won't be pourable, but is should be fairly thin and spreadable. If you find yours too thick, add another tablespoon of almond milk until it thins out a bit.

Sprinkle with chopped peanuts.

Makes 9 servings

Almond Flour French Toast

Ingredients

8 slices almond flour bread, about 1/2 inch thick
2 large eggs
1 tablespoon heavy cream
1/2 teaspoon ground cinnamon
2 teaspoon butter or coconut oil

Directions

Preheat oven to 200 degrees F.

Arrange slices of bread on a wire rack set over a baking sheet and place in oven. Let dry out for about 1 hr.

In a medium bowl, whisk together eggs, cream and cinnamon until well combined. Pour batter into a large shallow dish Place two slices of bread into and let sit 30 seconds to 1 minute to soak in mixture. Flip over and let sit another 30 to 1 minute seconds.

Meanwhile, heat a large, non-stick skillet over medium heat. Add butter and cook until butter just begins to brown, swirling to coat the bottom of the pan. Remove bread from batter and shake lightly to remove excess batter. Place in skillet and cook until golden brown on both sides, 2 to 3 minutes per side.

Transfer to wire rack and keep warm in oven while repeating with remaining bread.

Top with butter and sugar free syrup.

Almond Flour Bread

Ingredients

2 1/2 cups almond flour
1/2 cup oat fiber
1/4 cup unflavored whey protein powder
1 tablespoon granulated erythritol
2 teaspoon baking powder
1/2 teaspoon baking soda
1 teaspoon xanthan gum
1/2 teaspoon salt
6 oz Greek yogurt
6 tablespoon butter, softened
4 large eggs
6 tablespoon almond milk

Directions

Preheat oven to 325 degrees F and grease a 9x5 inch loaf pan.

In a medium bowl, whisk together the almond flour, oat fiber, whey protein, erythritol, baking powder, baking soda, xanthan gum and salt.

In a large bowl, beat together yogurt and butter until smooth. Beat in eggs, one at a time and scraping down bowl and beaters as needed. Add almond flour and beat until well combined. Beat in almond milk until thoroughly combined.

Spread batter in prepared loaf pan, smoothing the top. Bake 45 to 50 minutes, or until top is golden brown and a toothpick inserted in the center comes out clean. Let cool in pan 15 minutes, then flip onto a wire rack to cool completely.

Blackberry Lemon Ricotta Parfaits

This is a great summer breakfast but would be equally good as a dessert

Ingredients

15 oz whole milk ricotta
3 tablespoon fresh lemon juice
2 teaspoon lemon zest
2 tablespoon powdered erythritol
16 drops stevia extract
1 cup fresh blackberries
1/4 cup chopped toasted hazelnuts (optional)

Directions

Combine ricotta, lemon juice, lemon zest, erythritol and stevia in a food processor and process until very smooth, scraping down sides of bowl as needed, about 2 minutes.

Divide half of the berries among 6 dessert cups and top with half of ricotta mixture.

Repeat with remaining berries and remaining ricotta.

Sprinkle with chopped hazelnuts and serve.

Makes 6 servings

Crepes

Ingredients:
1 Egg
1/2 Packet of Splenda
1 teaspoon of water

Directions
In a small bowl combine egg, splenda, and water. Beat well until it becomes frothy.

Spray non stick pan with butter spray.

Pour 1/2 of the egg in to the middle of an omelet skillet.

Swirl around to make a circle.

Cook till ends start to lift up and are lacy brown.

Pick up the 2 ends with fingers lifting and turning the crepe over.

Cook both sides till crispy. Repeat so mixture makes crepes

Immediately top with all natural peanut butter or topping of your choice and enjoy.

Makes 1 servings

Sausage Egg Bake

Extreme Burn - Great recipe that can be assembled the day before and thrown in the oven the next morning

From Jen's Mom - Jane Matlas

Ingredients:

8 eggs
2 cups of Milk
1 lb. of ground sausage
8 oz package of shredded cheddar cheese

Directions

In a large skillet of medium high brown sausage. When completed drain fat.

In a bowl whisk the eggs and milk together.

Place sausage in 8x10 inch casserole dish pour eggs over it and then top with shredded cheese.

Bake at 350° F for 1 hour.

Makes 12 servings

Scotch Eggs

These can easily be stored in a zip top bag for at least a week.
They can be eaten plain or served with mustards.

Ingredients:
1 lb bulk pork sausage
1/2 cup shredded Parmesan cheese
6 hardboiled egg, peeled and dry

Directions:
Boil and remove the shells from 6 eggs. On a sheet of wax paper, spread out about 1/4 pound of the sausage and pat out thinly to about 3/8" thickness.

Sprinkle some grated cheese on top of the sausage and place one hardboiled egg in the center. Carefully wrap the sausage "blanket" around the egg keeping all the cheese on the inside. Make sure to pinch the sausage together where the ends meat to help keep the cheese inside. Repeat for the other three eggs.

Place them all on a baking sheet or in a baking pan and bake at 350°F for 30 minutes..

4

Snacks / Protein Grabs

Cottage Cheese, Black Bean and Avocado Salsa

Ingredients

1 (15-ounce) can whole kernel corn, drained
1 (15-ounce) can low-sodium black beans, drained and rinsed
1 (32-ounce) container fat-free cottage cheese
1 avocado, peeled, pitted and diced
2 tomatoes, diced
2 cups salsa
1/4 cup red onion, diced (optional)
1/4 cup cilantro, diced (optional)

Directions

Add all ingredients to a bowl and stir until blended.

Refrigerate until ready to serve.

Serve with low-fat tortilla chips or vegetables.

You can also use this as a filling for an omelet or add leftover cooked, diced chicken breast (or rotisserie chicken) and you have a complete meal.

Protein Microwave Brownie

Ingredients

1 egg
2 scoops Sweet Cream protein powder
1 tablespoon coco powder
2 tablespoon all natural peanut butter (no sugar added)
a bit of water

Directions

Mix all ingredients in small magic bullet mixing cup.

Pour mixture into a coffee mug.

Microwave on high for 1 minute.

Oven option: 425° F for 2 to 5 minutes

Makes 1 servings

Low Carb Herb & Cheese Crackers

Ingredients:
1/2 cup shredded cheese
1/4 cup almond meal
1/4 teaspoon garlic
1/4 teaspoon pepper

Directions
In a medium mixing bowl combine cheese, almond meal, garlic and pepper seasoning. Mix well.

Spread evenly on a cookie sheet lined with parchment paper.

Bake at 375° F for 15-20 min.

Cool before removing from pan.

Lift with a knife then cut or brake into pieces.

Pinwheels

Ingredients:

4 oz cream cheese, softened
4 oz chipped beef or ham
1 Tablespoon onion, grated
1 teaspoon Horseradish
Dash of Worcestershire sauce

Directions

Blend cream cheese, onion, horseradish, and Worcestershire sauce until of spreading consistency.

Carefully separate slices of Beef or Ham and spread with cheese mixture. Roll lengthwise and fasten with toothpicks.

Chill for at least an hour. Just before serving, slice into 1/2" slices.

Deviled Eggs

Ingredients
1 dozen eggs
2 teaspoons Dijon mustard
1/3 cup mayonnaise
Salt and pepper
Paprika

Directions
First hard boil the eggs. Fill up a large saucepan half-way with water and gently add the eggs. Cover the eggs with at least an inch of water. Add a teaspoon of vinegar to the water (this will help contain egg whites from leaking out if any of the shells crack while cooking). Add a pinch of salt to the water. Bring the water to a boil. Cover, and remove from heat. Let sit covered for 12-15 minutes. Drain hot water from pan and run cold water over the eggs. Let sit in the cool water a few minutes, changing the water if necessary to keep it cool.

Peel the eggs. Using a sharp knife, slice each egg in half, lengthwise. Gently remove the yolk halves and place in a small mixing bowl. Arrange the egg white halves on a serving platter.

Using a fork, mash up the yolks and add mustard, mayonnaise, and a sprinkling of salt and pepper. Spoon egg yolk mixture into the egg white halves. Sprinkle with paprika.

Ham-Wrapped Egg with Tuna

Recipe Submitted by Jen Scott

Ingredients

4 hard-boiled eggs, cooled
4 teaspoon mayonnaise (use light or olive oil style if desired)
3 tablespoon flaked tuna
2 or 3 thin slices of ham (I like to use prosciutto or serrano ham)
parsley for garnish
Salt to taste
Optional: 1 small clove garlic, minced or pressed.
8 Toothpicks

Directions

Boil eggs, let cool in refrigerator.

Peel, cut in half and remove yolks as for deviled eggs.

Mix yolks with mayonnaise, tuna, salt and garlic.

Cut bottoms of egg whites to sit level and spoon in tuna mixture.

Wrap sliced ham or prosciutto around egg halves and secure with toothpick.

Mug Muffin

A quick and easy morning protein grab for during Extreme Burn

Ingredients

1/4 cup Flax Seed Meal
1 teaspoon Butter (Melted)
1 teaspoon Splenda
1/2 teaspoon baking powder
1 teaspoon Cinnamon
1 Egg
1 Scoop Sweet Cream Protein Powder

Directions

Mix egg in a small dish and then add the melted butter.

In a coffee mug mix the dry ingredients (flax, Splenda, baking powder, cinnamon and protein powder).

Add wet ingredients to the dry ones in the mug and mix well.

Microwave the coffee mug for 2 minutes.

When timer goes off immediately remove and invert mug on plate. Enjoy!

Makes 1 serving

Tuna & Celery

Ingredients

1 - 6 oz. can of chunk light tuna in water
1 tablespoon low fat mayonnaise
4 celery stalks, cut in half
Emeril's Boyou Blast to taste

Directions

Drain the tuna and place in small mixing bowl.

Add mayonnaise and the seasoning to taste.

Mix well and then divide mixture evenly onto celery stalks.

Makes 4 servings.

Buffalo Chicken Dip

Great dip to use with celery during Extreme Burn

Recipe submitted by Natalie Martin

Ingredients

Chicken breast (2-3 cooked & shredded)
8 oz package of cream cheese
3/4 bottle of Ranch Dressing (or blue cheese dressing if you like)
Frank's Buffalo Hot Sauce (to your taste)

Directions

Preheat oven to 350° F.

In a large mixing bowl combine, cream cheese, dressing, and hot sauce. Mix together completely. Add chicken and toss to coat chicken.

Place mixture in a small casserole dish and bake in oven until cheese is melted and heated through about 20 to 30 minutes.

Serve with celery sticks.

Low Carb Cheesy Crackers

Recipe Submitted by Katy Gruner

Ingredients

1 Slice Kraft Deli Deluxe Cheese (I've only experimented with the American flavor)

Directions

Place slice of cheese on small square of parchment paper, leaving room on the edges because the cheese will expand...

Place in microwave for 45 seconds - 1 minute depending on strength of microwave.

Remove and cut into smaller, bite-size squares...Enjoy as all protein crispy cheese crackers!

Kale Chips

A good way to curb your appetite if you are craving a crispy, salty snack. These can be made ahead of time and stored for a few days in an airtight container but truthfully in our house they don't last very long once they come out of the oven.

Ingredients
1 bunch kale
1 tablespoon olive oil
1 teaspoon seasoned salt

Directions
Preheat an oven to 350° F.

Line a cookie sheet with parchment paper.

With a knife or kitchen shears carefully remove the leaves from the thick stems and tear into bite size pieces.

Wash and thoroughly dry kale with a salad spinner or by dabbing in paper towels. This is the most important step. If the Kale is too wet it won't become light and crispy and will burn before it does.

Drizzle kale with olive oil and sprinkle with seasoning salt. And gently toss together on cooking sheet.

Bake until the edges brown but are not burnt, 10 to 15 minutes.

Allow to cool for 5-10 minutes.

Cheesy Edamame

Ingredients

1 (12 ounce) package frozen shelled edamame (green soybeans)
1 tablespoon olive oil
1/4 cup grated Parmesan cheese
Salt and pepper to taste

Directions

Preheat the oven to 400° F.

Place the edamame into a colander and rinse under cold water to thaw. Drain thoroughly patting with a towel.

In a large bowl mix the oil, garlic, and cheese in a then add the edamame, tossing the ingredients together. Spread the edamame beans onto a cookie tray lined with parchment paper.

Bake in the preheated oven until the cheese is crispy and golden, about 15 minutes.

Edamame "Hummus"

This excellent served with celery or sliced cucumber.
15 Minutes to Prepare and Cook

Ingredients
1/2 pound frozen shelled edamame (green soy beans), about 1 1/2 cups
1/8 cup tahini
1/4 cup water
1/2 teaspoon freshly grated lemon zest
1 lemon (about 3 tablespoons), juiced
2 cloves garlic, minced
3/4 teaspoon kosher salt
1/2 teaspoon ground cumin
1/4 teaspoon ground coriander
1 1/2 tablespoons extra-virgin olive oil
1 tablespoon chopped fresh flat-leaf parsley

Directions

Boil the beans in salted water for 4 to 5 minutes, or microwave, covered, for 2 to 3 minutes.

In a food processor, puree the edamame, tahini, water, lemon zest and juice, garlic, salt, cumin, and coriander until smooth. With the motor running, slowly drizzle in 1 tablespoon of the olive oil and mix until absorbed.

Transfer to a small bowl, stir in the parsley and drizzle with remaining oil. Serve or refrigerate, covered, up to 1 day.

5

Sides

Parmesan Cauliflower

Ingredients

6 ounces cauliflower florets
2 teaspoons grated Parmesan
1 teaspoon fresh parsley (chopped)
1/4 teaspoon garlic powder
1/4 teaspoon ground pepper
Salt to taste
1 teaspoon extra virgin olive oil

Directions

Preheat the oven to 425° F.

Combine all the ingredients except the oil into a bowl and toss well. Then add the oil into the bowl and gently toss. Place on a nonstick backing dish.

Bake for 15 to 17 minutes or until lightly browned, tossing half way through the baking time. Can be served as soon as removed from the oven.

Makes 2 servings

Cauliflower Hash Browns

Serve these with your Eggs & Bacon and you won't miss those other ones.

Ingredients

12 ounces grated fresh cauliflower (about 1/2 a medium)
4 slices bacon, chopped
3 ounces chopped onion (about 1/2 cup)*
1-2 tablespoons butter (optional)
Salt and pepper, to taste

Directions

In a medium-large nonstick skillet, cook the bacon and onion until they just start to brown.

Add the cauliflower; cook and stir until the cauliflower is tender and nicely browned all over.

You can add a couple tablespoons of butter during cooking. This will speed up the browning and add nice flavor.

Season to taste with salt and pepper.

Makes 4 servings

Zucchini And Mushroom "Noodles"

Ingredients:
3 medium zucchini
8 ounces fresh mushrooms, sliced
1 1/2 tablespoons butter
1/3 cup heavy cream
1/2 cup Parmesan cheese, 2 ounces
Salt and pepper, to taste
1/4 teaspoon garlic powder

Directions:
Cut the blossom end off each zucchini. Then, while holding the stem end, run a vegetable peeler down the length of the zucchini to remove a thin strip of the peel. Continue cutting "ribbons" in this manner. Once you've worked your way all the way around the squash, discard the inner seed core.

Heat the butter in a large skillet over medium-high heat. Add the mushrooms and cook until all of the liquid has evaporated. Add the cream and Parmesan. Simmer until the sauce has thickened. Stir in the zucchini and cook just until tender. Season with salt, pepper and garlic powder.

Makes 4-6 servings

Cauliflower "Potato" Salad

Prep time: 40 minutes

Ingredients

3 hard-boiled eggs
1 large head of cauliflower, washed and outer leaves trimmed off
1/3 cup light mayonnaise
1/3 cup buttermilk
3/4 cup low-fat cottage cheese
1 generous tablespoon good mustard
2 tablespoons sweet relish
1 carrot, peeled and grated
1/2 a large onion, chopped fine or grated with a box cutter
3 ribs celery, chopped on the diagonal
Fresh herbs, dill is great, oregano is good too
Salt & pepper to taste

Directions

Grate the cauliflower on the large holes of cheese grater. Heat a large skillet on medium high, add the water. Drop in the cauliflower and cook, stirring often, adding water as needed, until the cauliflower's rawness is cooked out, and it becomes slightly tender seasoning with salt along the way. Be generous with the salt in this stage and don't let the cauliflower get brown. Allow the cauliflower to cool.

In a large mixing bowl combine cooked cauliflower, eggs (roughly mashed with a fork) carrot, onion, celery, and dill.

Meanwhile, in a small bowl, whisk together the dressing ingredients, mayonnaise, buttermilk, cottage cheese, mustard, and relish.

Pour the mixed dressing over the cauliflower mixture. Taste and season with salt & pepper to taste.

If time allows, cover and refrigerate for two to 24 hours, allowing the flavors to combine.

Green Beans with Almond Slivers

Ingredients

1 cup thin green beans
3 shallots, sliced thin
1 tablespoon olive oil
1 teaspoon white wine vinegar
1 teaspoon maple syrup
1/4 cup slivered almonds
Salt and pepper to taste if desired

Directions

Steam the green beans until bright green.

Meanwhile in a large pan sauté the shallots in the olive oil, vinegar and maple syrup until translucent.

Add in the almonds until they start to brown.

Add the steamed green beans to the pan and toss gently.

Serve immediately.

Makes 2 servings

Parmesan Grilled Asparagus

Ingredients

Olive oil cooking spray
1 pound fresh asparagus, tough ends trimmed
1/4 cup shredded Parmesan cheese
1 teaspoon sea salt
1/4 teaspoon garlic powder, or to taste

Directions

Preheat oven to 400°

Spray the inside of a 9x13 casserole dish with olive oil cooking spray.

Place asparagus in the dish and lightly spray spears with cooking spray.

Sprinkle asparagus with Parmesan cheese, sea salt, and garlic powder.

Roast in preheated oven until fork easily punctures thickest part of stem, about 12 minutes.

Makes 4 Servings

Grilled Romaine Salad

Ingredients
3 romaine hearts
1 teaspoon olive oil (for grill)
1/4 cup crumbled blue cheese
1/4 cup crumbled bacon
1/2 cup extra virgin olive oil
1/4 cup balsamic vinegar

Directions
In a small bowl mix together blue cheese, bacon, extra virgin olive oil, and balsamic vinegar. Set aside.

Preheat a grill or grill pan to a medium heat.

Wash and dry your lettuce. Make sure the romaine is totally dry before you grill it or you will end up with a soggy salad. Do not trim the end, that is what holds the lettuce together. Simple slice the romaine heart in half.

Place cut-side down on an oiled grill or grill pan. Cook for 2-3 minutes each side. Don't leave it on for too long or it will lose all of it's crunch.

Place the romaine cut-side up on a plate.. Serve immediately!

Makes 6 Servings

Cucumber Salad

This is a low carb take on one of my favorite fresh tasting light summer salads,. It tastes even better after sitting a day so it is a great recipe to make and eat off of the whole week.

Ingredients

3 medium cucumbers
1/2 medium white onion
3 cups cold water
1 1/2 cup white vinegar
2/3 teaspoon Splenda
Salt and pepper to taste

Directions

Slice cucumbers into super thin rounds.

Finely sliver the onion slices.

In a container with a lid combine all of the ingredients and stir well.

Place container covered into the fridge and allow to sit for at least 4 hours but up to 5 days.

Makes 6 servings

Stuffed Mushrooms

Ingredients

4 medium button mushrooms
1/2 ounce fat-free crumbled feta cheese
2 teaspoons fresh parsley (chopped)
1/2 teaspoon extra virgin olive oil
Pinch cayenne pepper

Directions

Preheat the oven to 425 degrees F. Spray a non stick backing dish with cooking spray such as olive oil Pam.

Twist the stems on the mushrooms so that it come clean from them leaving only the empty top. Reserve the stems. Place the mushroom caps into the baking dish stem side up.

Finely chop the reserve stems and place into a small mixing bowl. Add the feta, parsley, oil, and cayenne pepper and mix together well. Spoon the mixture into the mushrooms caps dividing it evenly filling each of them creating a small mound.

Bake for 12 to 15 minutes or until tender. Let stand 5 minutes before serving.

Makes 1 serving.

Caesar Salad

This excellent served with grilled chicken or lemon pepper shrimp.
5 Minutes to Prepare and Cook

Ingredients
1/4 cup pasteurized egg substitute
1 clove of garlic, minced
1 1/2 teaspoon anchovy paste
1/2 teaspoon Dijon mustard
1/2 teaspoon Worcestershire sauce
2 tablespoons fresh lemon juice
2 tablespoons extra virgin olive oil
1/4 cup grated Parmesan cheese
Salt and freshly ground pepper
8 cups torn romaine lettuce

Directions
In a small mixing bowl, whisk together egg substitute, garlic, anchovy, mustard, Worcestershire sauce and lemon juice.

Slowly add in the olive oil whisking the mix continuously as you pour. Add in the Parmesan cheese and then add the salt and pepper to taste.

In a large bowl toss the dressing with lettuce and protein (chicken breast etc.) if you choose.

Makes 4 servings.

Lemon-Nut Kale

Ingredients
1 lb fresh kale, removed from woody stems and chopped
1 large garlic clove, crushed
1 tablespoons extra virgin olive oil
juice of 1 lemon
2 tablespoons pine nuts, lightly toasted

Directions
Add oil to a large skillet over medium heat.

Add garlic when oil is hot and toss together for a few seconds.

Add kale and saute until tender, about 10 minutes.

Remove pan from heat, stir in lemon juice and top with pine nuts to serve.

Balsamic Broccoli

15 Minutes to Prepare and Cook

Ingredients:

1 1/2 lbs broccoli florets
2 tablespoons extra virgin olive oil
1 tablespoon lemon juice
1 tablespoon balsamic vinegar
Lemon wedge
Salt and pepper

Directions:

In a steamer, place the broccoli and cook over simmering water for 10 minutes or until fork tender.

Mix together the oil, lemon juice, and vinegar, and drizzle over; garnish with lemon wedges and season with salt and pepper.

Makes 4 servings

Caprese Salad

15 Minutes to Prepare and Cook

Ingredients:

3 vine-ripe tomatoes, 1/4-inch thick slices
1 pound fresh mozzarella, 1/4-inch thick slices
20 to 30 leaves (about 1 bunch) fresh basil
Extra-virgin olive oil, for drizzling
Balsamic Vinegar For Drizzling
Coarse salt and pepper

Directions:

Layer alternating slices of tomatoes and mozzarella, adding a basil leaf between each, on a large, shallow platter.

Drizzle the salad with extra-virgin olive oil followed by balsamic vinegar and season with salt and pepper, to taste.

Makes 4 servings.

6

Main Dishes

Quick 'N Easy Balsamic Chicken

High Protein, Low Fat Heart-Healthy Food Option

25 Minutes to Prepare and Cook

Ingredients

1 Chicken Breast (cut in thin 2-inch strips)
4 Tablespoon Balsamic Vinegar
2 teaspoon freshly chopped garlic
1 teaspoon Olive Oil
Salt and Pepper to taste

Directions

Cut chicken breast in thin 2-inch strips

Chop fresh garlic - about 2 teaspoon (about 4-5 cloves of garlic)

Heat oil in a pan and add garlic. Saute until golden.

Add chicken and stir well.

Add Balsamic vinegar and salt and pepper.

Reduce the heat to medium and let the excess water evaporate.

Keep stirring intermittently, making sure that all the water dries up and the chicken is well coated with Balsamic Vinegar.

Serve hot with some brown rice or whole wheat pasta.

Easy Turkey Chili

Done in less than 30 minutes and super healthy

45 Minutes to Prepare and Cook

Ingredients

1 pound lean ground turkey (93% lean)
2C chopped onion
1 cup chopped celery
1 cup chopped bell pepper
6 cloves chopped garlic
2 tablespoon olive oil
1 can black beans
2 can kidney beans
1 can pinto beans
2 cans diced tomatoes
1 quart chicken broth
Chili powder to taste

Directions

Brown ground turkey in 1 tablespoon olive oil, sauté onion, celery, bell pepper and garlic in 1 tablespoon olive oil.

Add remaining ingredients and simmer for 15 minutes or longer to taste.

Add chili powder, salt, and pepper to taste.

Makes 8 Servings

Crock Pot Pizza Chicken

Ingredients

8 boneless, skinless chicken breasts
1/4 teaspoon salt
1/4 teaspoon pepper
1 chopped onion
2 green bell peppers, cut into 1" pieces
2 cup jarred pizza sauce (watch the sugar, I use Trader Joe's brand)
1 cup shredded mozzarella cheese

Directions

Sprinkle chicken with salt and pepper.

Place in a 3 - 4 quart crock pot/slow cooker.

Top with the onions and bell pepper.

Pour the pizza sauce over all.

Cover and cook on low for 4 - 5 hours, until chicken is thoroughly cooked.

Stir well.

Sprinkle with cheese and let stand 5 minutes to melt cheese.

Makes 8 servings.

Herb Grilled Chicken

Ingredients

2 tablespoons chopped Italian flat leaf parsley
2 teaspoons fresh rosemary, minced
2 teaspoons chopped fresh thyme
1 teaspoon dried sage
3 cloves garlic, minced
1/4 cup olive oil
1/3 cup balsamic vinegar
Salt and pepper to taste
1 1/2 pounds skinless, boneless chicken breasts

Directions

In a blender cup or small food processer combine the parsley, rosemary, thyme, sage, garlic, oil, vinegar and salt and pepper to taste. Blend together.

Place chicken in a nonporous glass dish or bowl and pour blended marinade over the chicken. Cover dish and refrigerate to marinate for at least 2 hours or overnight.

Preheat grill to medium high heat. Remove chicken from dish and dispose of leftover marinade. Grill for about 6 to 7 minutes per side, or until chicken is cooked through and no longer pink inside.

Mexican Chicken

My favorite after workout meal

15 Minutes to Prepare and Cook

Ingredients

2 6-8 oz chicken breasts
1 Tablespoon taco seasoning
4 oz shredded cheddar or Mexican cheese blend
1/2 avocado

Directions

Preheat grill pan to medium-high heat.

Coat the chicken in the taco seasoning. Cook for 5-7 minutes per side.

Top each chicken breast with the cheese in the last 2 minutes of cooking so it melts over the chicken.

Remove from heat and place 1 to 2 slices of avocado over the chicken.

Makes 1 Serving

Enchilada Chicken

15 Minutes to Prepare and Cook

Ingredients

4 - 4 oz chicken breasts
2 teaspoons taco seasoning
4 tablespoons mild, medium or hot enchilada sauce
2 oz shredded cheddar or Mexican cheese blend
2 tablespoons finely chopped fresh cilantro

Directions

Preheat oven to 350° F.

Season each chicken breast with the taco seasoning on all sides.

Using a large oven proof skillet. Lightly mist with cooking spray and then cook chicken for 1-2 minutes on each side or just until the chicken becomes brown.

Remove the pan from heat and top each chicken breast with 1 teaspoon of enchilada sauce, then the cheese and cilantro.

Place pan in the oven for 4 to 6 minutes or until the chicken is no longer pink inside and the cheese is melted.

Makes 4 Servings

Dijon Chicken

20 Minutes to Prepare and Cook

Ingredients

1/4 cup and 1 tablespoon Dijon mustard
2 tablespoon white wine (such as Chardonnay)
1/4 teaspoon Worcestershire sauce
Black pepper to taste (ground)
2 tablespoon finely minced shallot
3 tablespoon pure maple syrup (Grade B or higher)
4 - 4 oz. boneless, skinless chicken breasts

Directions

In a large shallow dish mix, the 1/4 cup mustard, wine, Worcestershire sauce, pepper and 1 tablespoon maple syrup. Place the chicken into the dish, being sure to turn it to evenly coat it and let stand for 5 minutes to allow it to marinate. You may also cover and refrigerate if you wish to prep ahead of time. Preheat a ridged grill pan or grill. Remove chicken discarding any remaining marinade. Grill on each side for 3 to 5 minutes or until chicken is no longer pink in the middle.

Meanwhile in a small bowl, combine the remaining ingredients, 2 tablespoon maple syrup, 1 tablespoon mustard, and 1 tablespoon shallot. Mix together well and serve as a dipping sauce for the finished chicken.

Makes 4 servings

Spicy Chicken & Spinach Casserole

Ingredients

3 cups cooked, diced chicken
10 ounce package frozen chopped spinach, thawed and drained well
1 small onion, chopped
1 tablespoon butter
1/4 cup canned pickled jalapeños, roughly chopped,
1 ounce can
8 ounces cream cheese, softened
1/3 cup sour cream
10 ounce can Ro-tel tomatoes, drained (tomatoes with green chilies)
1/4 teaspoon cumin
1/2 teaspoon chili powder
8 ounces cheddar cheese, shredded

Directions

Preheat over to 350° F

Mix the chicken and spinach in a greased 2 1/2 quart casserole.

Meanwhile, sauté the onion in butter until tender; add to the chicken.

Stir in all of the remaining ingredients and mix well. Season with salt and pepper, to taste.

Bake, uncovered, 40-50 minutes, until hot and bubbly.

Chicken Basil Meatloaf

Prep and Cook time: 35 min

Ingredients:

1lb Ground Chicken
1 egg, whisked
1/2 cup almond flour/meal
1/2 cup fresh basil, chopped
1/2 tablespoon garlic powder
1/2 tablespoon onion powder
1/2 teaspoon dried parsley
salt and pepper, to taste

Directions:

Preheat oven to 375 degrees.

Mix together all ingredients for meatloaf in a bowl.

Place ingredients into a lightly greased loaf pan.

Bake for 25-30 minutes or until there is no pink remaining in the loaf.

Makes 3-4 Servings

Asparagus, Tomato, Chicken and Penne Pasta

Ingredients

1 (16 ounce) package whole-wheat penne pasta
1 pound skinless, boneless chicken breast, cut into bite-size pieces
1/4 teaspoon salt
1/4 teaspoon pepper
2 tablespoons olive oil, divided
2 teaspoons bottled, minced garlic
1 cup low-sodium chicken broth
12 ounces asparagus, trimmed and cut into 1-inch pieces
1 cup cherry tomatoes, diced
1 teaspoon crushed red pepper flakes
1/2 cup non-fat Parmesan cheese

Directions

Cook pasta according to directions, drain and transfer to a large bowl. While pasta cooks, heat olive oil in a large nonstick skillet over medium heat. Season chicken with salt and pepper and sauté until no longer pink in the middle.

Remove from pan. Add remaining tablespoon of olive oil and sauté garlic for a few seconds. Add chicken broth and bring to a boil. Add asparagus, tomatoes and red pepper flakes and cook until asparagus is tender. Stir in chicken and cook for two minutes. Toss pasta with chicken and vegetables and sprinkle with Parmesan cheese.

Makes 6-8 servings

Awesome Southwest Tortilla Soup

Ingredients

3 chicken breasts (grilled or steamed)
2 green zucchini (cut into spoon-size pieces)
2 yellow squash (cut into spoon-size pieces)
1 yellow onion (diced)
5 garlic cloves, minced
6 medium red tomatoes (diced into spoon-size pieces)
3 medium tomatoes, pureed
½ bunch cilantro (fresh, washed, then chopped)
2 tablespoon chili powder
1 tablespoon cumin
1 teaspoon cayenne red pepper
2 teaspoon salt
2 teaspoon black pepper

Directions

Shred the cooked chicken into a pot and add zucchini, squash, diced tomatoes, pureed tomatoes and cilantro. Fill the pot about 2 inches from top with water. Add chili powder, cumin, cayenne pepper, salt and black pepper.

Cook at medium heat for approximately one hour or until vegetables are tender and soup has reached full boil for 20 minutes. Makes one large cooking pot.

You may also add a slice of avocado diced over the top just prior to serving if you have not exceeded your daily fat intake for the day. Add additional chili powder, cumin, and cayenne red pepper according to your tolerance for spiciness.

Makes 6-8 servings

Bruschetta Quinoa

Great Smart Meal!

Recipe Submitted by Terri Nolan

Ingredients

1 cup quinoa (uncooked) - make sure to get pre-rinsed, otherwise you'll need to rinse to get rid of the bitter flavor
1 can cannelloni beans
1 cup store bought tomato bruschetta or diced tomatoes (low sodium)
4 ounce can of mushrooms, diced small
1/4 of a white onion, diced
1 green pepper, diced
2 cloves garlic, minced
1/4 cup balsamic vinegar (optional)
1/4 cup grated Parmesan cheese
2 chicken breasts
Head of broccoli (as much you want)

Directions

Cook the chicken as normal. We cook the quinoa as directed (either with water or chicken broth).

As quinoa is cooking (about 15 minutes), sauté the veggies (except the tomatoes) with Italian seasonings and olive oil spray or a little extra virgin olive oil.

Add the beans and vinegar when the veggies are the right consistency. Toss the quinoa/chicken in a bowl with the cheese and veggie/bean mixture.

Then, add the cold bruschetta mix (to prevent from cooking the tomatoes) and toss. Drizzle with balsamic glaze.

Variations

Add red pepper flakes, a dash of sriracha (hot chili sauce), and a dash of stevia for a sweet and spicy flavor.

Change beans/veggies to different combos (i.e Mexican = black beans, corn, rotel tomatoes)

Asian Chicken and Macaroni Salad

Ingredients

1 package Macaroni Shirataki
4 cooked skinless boneless chicken breasts, diced
1 1/4 cups bean sprouts
1 1/2 cups snow peas
1/4 cup chopped scallions
1/4 cup vegetable oil
5 teaspoons soy sauce
1 teaspoon ground ginger
1/8 teaspoon salt
1/8 teaspoon freshly ground black pepper
1/8 teaspoon sugar
1/4 cup diced celery
1 (8-ounce) can sliced water chestnuts, drained

Directions

Drain and rinse Shirataki Noodles very well. Place on paper towels to dry and set aside.

Combine the chicken, bean sprouts, snow peas,Macaroni Shirataki and scallions.

Make a dressing using the oil, soy sauce, ginger, salt, pepper, and sugar.

Add to the chicken mixture. Add the celery and water chestnuts and mix well.

Serve chilled.

Meat Muffins

Great Extreme Burn recipe!

Ingredients

1 Egg
1 lb. of ground turkey
1 cup uncooked oatmeal
1 onion (chopped)
1 carrot (shredded)
1/3 cup Ketchup
1/4 cup shredded Parmesan cheese (plus additional for topping)
1 teaspoon salt
1/4 teaspoon fresh ground pepper

Directions

Preheat oven to 350° F. Spray muffin tin with non stick cooking spray.

In a large bowl combine all the ingredients together. Using you hands is best to really mix thoroughly.

Divide the mixture into 8-10 balls placing each ball into a muffin spot of the tin and press down lightly.

Bake for 15-20 minutes.

Place additional Parmesan cheese onto of each muffin and place back into the oven for 5 minutes or until meat is no longer pink in the middle

Makes 8-10 servings

Low Carb, High Protein Taco Bake

You can serve with additional toppings like shredded lettuce, jalapenos, guacamole, ripe olives, sour cream or salsa, but be sure to add in your nutrition info.

Ingredients

Crust

- 4 ounces fat free cream cheese, softened
- 3 egg whites
- 1/3 cup Fat free half and half
- 1/2 teaspoon taco seasoning
- 8 ounces low fat cheddar cheese, shredded

Topping

- 1 lb. ground turkey, 93% lean
- 3 teaspoons taco seasoning
- 1/4 cup tomato sauce
- 4 ounces chopped green chilies
- 8 ounces cheddar cheese, shredded

Directions

Preheat oven to 375° F.

For the crust, beat the cream cheese and eggs until smooth. Add the cream and seasoning.

Grease a 9"x13" baking dish; spread the cheese over the bottom. Pour in the egg mixture as evenly as possible.

Bake at 375° F, 25-30 minutes. Let stand 5 minutes before adding the topping.

For the topping, brown the hamburger; drain fat.
Stir in the seasoning, tomato sauce and chiles. Spread over the crust. Top with cheese.

Reduce oven to 350° F and bake another 20 minutes or so until hot and bubbly.

Serve with the toppings of your choice (add additional carbs).

Makes 8 servings.

Turkey Soufflé

(Protein or meal day) Ideal Protein day if you take the flour out.
Filling low carb, high-protein meal!

Ingredients

2 cups fresh turkey breast meat - cubed
9 medium eggs, whites/yolks separated
9 tablespoon whole wheat flour
9 tablespoon margarine
1 teaspoon black pepper
1 teaspoon salt

Directions

Melt margarine in at least a 2 qt saucepan and slowly add flour, stirring constantly until mixture is creamy. Turn off stove.

Slowly add egg yolks and whites continue stirring as the mixture cools slightly. Stir in cubed turkey breast meat until thoroughly mixed. Pour mixture into a greased 4-6 qt. baking dish.

Bake uncovered at 350° for 45 minutes, or until the top is slightly browned and/or a knife comes out clean from the center of the soufflé.

Make 12 servings

Crock Pot Beef And Peppers

Ingredients

3 to 4 lb. Round steak lean
2 Green peppers sliced thin
1/2 cup onions minced
2 cup Beef broth
3 tablespoon soy sauce
1/2 teaspoon Ground ginger
1 Garlic clove -- minced
1 teaspoon Worcestershire sauce

Directions

Cut the steak into serving size pieces. If desired you can brown the meat in a little hot oil before adding to crock pot.

Place the thinly sliced pepper rings in bottom of crock pot, reserving a few to place on top of meat if desired.

Arrange the meat on pepper, careful to not stack one piece directly on top of another.

Mix all other ingredients and pour over meat and peppers.

Cover and cook on low for 8-10 hours or on high for about 4 hours.

Crock Pot Meatballs

Ingredients:
4 cloves of garlic
1/4 onion divided in two portions
1 egg
1.5 pounds of ground beef
1/4 cup Parmesan cheese
Dried parsley (to taste)
Dried red pepper flakes (to taste)
1 can tomato sauce
1/2 teaspoon garlic powder
1/4 teaspoon dried onion
1/2 teaspoon dried oregano
1 teaspoon liquid Splenda

Directions:
Use a food processor to blend egg 2 cloves of garlic and one portion of the onion until they are all liquid.

In a large mixing bowl mix the egg mixture, beef, cheese, parsley, and red pepper.

Form the beef into meatballs slightly smaller than golf balls and fry them in olive oil until just browned on the outside (not cooked through). Place the meatballs in the crock pot.

Mix the tomatoes sauce with the remaining onion, two crushed garlic cloves, oregano, garlic powder, dried onion, and a about a teaspoon of sweetener (adjust all seasonings to taste). Pour this over the meatballs.

Cook on low for 8 hours.

There will be lots of fat floating in the sauce when these are done. So after the first time you eat them put the meatballs in one storage container and the sauce in another, then refrigerate, once the sauce cools you will be able to scrape the fat off the top and you will be left with a thicker tasty sauce to pour over the meatballs. These are great reheated and make an easy microwave lunch you can even top them with shredded mozzarella.

Sloppy Joe Stuffed Peppers

Ingredients
1 pound ground beef
1 ounce onion, chopped, about 2 tablespoons
1 stalk celery, chopped
1 clove garlic, minced
1/2 cup tomato sauce
1 teaspoon granular Splenda
1 1/2 teaspoons white vinegar
1 1/2 teaspoons Worcestershire sauce
1/2 teaspoon mustard
1/2 teaspoon salt
1/8 teaspoon pepper
8 ounces cheddar cheese, shredded
3 green peppers, halved lengthwise

Directions
Preheat over to 350° F
Brown the ground beef, onion, celery and garlic; drain the fat. Stir in all of the remaining ingredients except the cheese and green peppers. Simmer 10 minutes.

Meanwhile, parboil the peppers in a little boiling water 3 minutes; drain. Place the peppers in a baking dish. Stir half of the cheese into the hamburger mixture; fill the peppers with the meat. Top with the remaining cheese. Bake for 15-20 minutes until hot and bubbly and the peppers are tender.

Makes 6 servings

Chili Taco Salad

Ingredients

1 onion, finely chopped
1 teaspoon bottled, minced garlic
1 pound lean ground turkey or lean ground beef
2 tablespoons chili powder
2 teaspoons cumin
1/4 teaspoon crushed red pepper
1 (19 ounce) can kidney beans, rinsed and drained
2 cups salsa
2 cups shredded lettuce
2 cups tomatoes, diced
1/2 cup black olives
1 cup low-fat shredded Mexican cheese
Cooking spray

Preparation

Spray a nonstick skillet with cooking spray and sauté onion and garlic over medium high heat. Cook for about five minutes or until onion is translucent.

Add the meat and cook until no longer pink. Add chili powder, cumin, red pepper, kidney beans and salsa and cook over medium heat for about five minutes.

Divide lettuce and tomatoes among four plates. Add the meat mixture and top with black olives and cheese.

Makes 4 servings

Fake Out Lasagna

It tastes as close to lasagna as you can get without noodles!

Ingredients

2 large zucchini, peeled and cut lengthwise
1 small can tomato sauce
8 oz ricotta cheese
6 oz shredded mozzarella
1 lb. Italian sausage or hamburger, cooked and drained
Garlic salt

Directions

Preheat oven to 350° F.

Cover bottom of small glass pan with 1/3 tomato sauce.

Place several slices of zucchini on top.

Layer meat cheeses seasoning more sauce.

Put more zucchini on top and layer again.

Top with last bit of mozzarella.

Bake for about 45 min.

Makes 8 servings

Corned Beef and Cabbage

Ingredients

1 Corned Beef brisket

1 1/2 cups water

Seasoning Packet -may come with corned beef, if not

  2 bay leaves

  Tablespoon peppercorns

  Salt as desired

1/2 head green cabbage, cut in serving size wedges

Directions

Place brisket, water and seasoning into the crock pot.

Cook on low for about 6 hours.

Add cabbage wedges and cook for 2 more hours.

Crustless Pizza

Great Extreme Burn recipe for when you want the flavor of pizza without all of the carbs!

Ingredients
2 lbs of ground beef (ground round is best)
2 whole eggs
1 jar of pizza sauce (I like Trader Joe's brand one as it's lower in carbs)
16 oz of shredded mozzarella
1 package of pepperoni

Directions
Preheat oven to 350° F.

Brown the ground beef in a large skillet until it is mostly cooked all the way through. Drain meat.

Beat together eggs in a small dish and mix together with meat.

Spray a 11x13 inch dish with non-stick cooking spray.

Pat the meat and egg mixture in to the pan and press down well.

Pour jar of pizza sauce over it spreading to cover meat. Top with mozzarella cheese and then pepperoni.

Bake for 30 minutes.

Makes 6-8 servings

You may also ut this recipe in half and use a 9 inch pie dish.

Mini Spinach Meatloaf

Recipe submitted by Flo Woodring

Ingredients

1 lb. lean ground beef
1 lb. ground turkey
2 eggs
2 cloves of pressed garlic (add to your liking)
1-2 cups of finely chopped spinach
1/4 cup dried vegetable flakes
1 tablespoon Italian seasoning
Salt and pepper (optional)
Shredded Sharp Cheese (for top of meatloaf's)
Parsley (top garnish)

Directions

Mix together, form into mini meatloaf's and bake at 350 degrees for about 45 minutes. May need time adjustment if making a bigger one.

Tips

For an smart meal, add 1 cup of cooked Quinoa..

Form into meatballs and bake at 400 degrees for 20 - 30 minutes, then freeze when cooled. Use for an all protein meal, put frozen meatballs into crock pot with bbq sauce about 4-5 hours on low.

Crock Pot Soy Sauce Ribs

Ingredients
2 lbs country pork ribs (cut into 3-4 pieces each)
1/4 cup soy sauce
1-2 garlic cloves crushed
1/4 inch piece fresh ginger chopped
1/2 tablespoon toasted sesame oil

Directions
Place ribs into crock pot

In a small bowl mix together soy sauce, garlic, ginger and oil. Pour over the ribs.

Cook for 3-4 hours on high, 5-6 on low and the meat just fall off the bone.

Crock Pot Carnitas

One of may favorite "smart mea;" dishes is a burrito bowl from Chipotle. Here you can make your own Carnitas on the weekend and then during the week assemble it into a burrito bowl with brown rice or make into a salad on an alternating day.

Ingredients
3 lb. boneless pork roast (shoulder or butt), cut into bite size strips
1/2 cup water
2 minced cloves garlic or 2 teaspoon garlic powder
1 cup chopped onion
1 teaspoon salt
1/2 teaspoon each: black pepper; cumin; oregano; lemon pepper
1/4 teaspoon cayenne

Directions
Combine ingredients in crock pot.

Cook on high 1 hour, then low 8 hours.

Remove pork with slotted spoon.

Pour liquid into a nonstick skillet and boil down to about 1/2 cup.

Add pork and saute until browned.

Grilled Salmon

High in protein, low in carbs and calories!

1 hour to Prepare and Cook

Ingredients

2 tablespoons extra virgin olive oil
1 teaspoon water
1/2 cup red wine vinegar
2 cloves garlic minced
1 teaspoon garlic salt
1/2 teaspoon freshly ground black pepper
2 teaspoons dried basil
5 oz. Salmon fillet

Directions

Preheat an outdoor grill for medium heat and lightly oil grate.

In a shallow baking pan, combine the olive oil, water, red wine vinegar, garlic, garlic salt, black pepper and basil. Place salmon filet in the marinade meat side down, if skin is still on. Marinate for 30 minutes. Can also be done ahead of time and refrigerated overnight.

Place on grill and cook 12 minutes per side. Baste with marinade periodically while cooking. Salmon is done, when it flakes easily with a fork.

Makes 1 serving

Salmon Salad

High in protein, low in carbs and calories!

5 Minutes to Prepare and Cook

Ingredients

2 cups salmon, flaked
1 red or yellow bell pepper, diced
1 cucumber, peeled, seeded & diced
.5 cup chopped onion
4-5 tablespoon greek yogurt, plain (enough to moisten)
1/4 teaspoon cayenne pepper
Salt & pepper
Juice of 1/2 a lemon
*Optional: 2 hardboiled eggs (not included in nutritional information)

Directions

In a large bowl, gently toss together the salmon and crushed hard-boiled eggs (optional).

In another bowl, combine bell pepper, cucumber, onion, and yogurt. Add seasonings and stir to combine.

Pour mixture over salmon, add lemon juice, and toss lightly to combine. Serve over lettuce or as a sandwich.

Makes 4 servings

Slammin' Salmon

Packed with flavor this grilled salmon will tempt your taste buds.

20 Minutes to Prepare and Cook (not including marinating time)

Ingredients

1/4 cup balsamic vinegar
1/4 cup lemon juice
1/4 cup soy sauce
1 teaspoon salt
1 tablespoon brown sugar
1 1/2 teaspoons ground ginger
1 teaspoon paprika
1 teaspoon black pepper
1 teaspoon crushed red pepper flakes
4 cloves garlic, minced
1/4 cup chopped green onions
1 teaspoon sesame oil
8 (4 ounce) skinless, boneless salmon fillets

Directions

Stir balsamic vinegar, lemon juice, and soy sauce with salt, brown sugar, ground ginger, paprika, pepper, and red pepper flakes until the salt has dissolved. Stir in garlic, green onions, and sesame oil until well combined. Pour marinade into a plastic storage bag or glass bowl. Add salmon to marinade and gently toss to coat. Place into refrigerator and marinate 2 to 24 hours.

Prepare an outdoor grill or gill pan for medium-high heat. Remove salmon fillets from marinade and grill until firm and opaque, about 4 minutes per side.

Makes 4 servings

Tuna Patty Melt

Low fat/calorie, high protein alternative to a beef or chicken burger.
15 Minutes to Prepare and Cook

Ingredients
1 Can of Tuna (drained)
1 Egg White
1/3 Cup of Low Fat Cheddar Cheese
1/2 Small Onion (Finely Chopped)
1 teaspoon Ground Garlic
1/2 teaspoon Pepper

Directions
In a bowl mix drained tuna, egg white, cheese, onion and spices until all the ingredients stick together.

Split in half and form two patties.

In a medium saucepan, fry patties until both sides are golden brown.

Makes 2 servings

Lemon Pepper Shrimp

10 Minutes to Prepare and Cook

Ingredients

1 lb.. large shrimp, peeled & deveined
2 teaspoons extra virgin olive oil
1/2 teaspoon salt
1/2 teaspoon coarsely ground pepper
1/2 teaspoon lemon zest, finely grated
3 tablespoons fresh lemon juice

Directions

Preheat a grill pan over medium-high heat.

Toss the shrimp with the oil.

Add the salt, pepper and lemon zest and toss again.

Grill for 2-3 minutes each side.

Remove shrimp to a plate and sprinkle with the lemon juice.

Makes 4 servings

Shrimp Lettuce Wraps

15 Minutes to Prepare and Cook

Ingredients

2 tablespoons low fat mayonnaise
2 tablespoons low fat plain greek yogurt
2 teaspoons lemon juice
2 tablespoons Emeril's Essence Creole Seasoning
1 pound cooked, peeled and deveined shrimp
12 Bibb lettuce leaves

Directions

In a large mixing bowl mix the mayonnaise, yogurt, lemon juice, and seasoning until completely mixed. Add the shrimp and toss until shrimp is well coated.

Evenly divide the shrimp mixture onto the middle of the lettuce leaves. Serve immediately.

Makes 4 servings

Low Carb Tuna Casserole

Ingredients
1/2 stick butter (4 Tablespoons)
1 pkg (8 oz) cream cheese
3/4 cup whipping cream
2 cans (9 oz. ea.) Chunk tuna in spring water, drained
1/3 cup chopped green pepper
1/2 chopped onion
2 oz. jar diced pimientos, drained
1-1/2 cups frozen green beans
1 cup shredded Cheddar/Monterey cheese
1/2 cup grated Parmesan cheese
2 Tablespoons dried parsley
pinch dried tarragon
pinch dried thyme
Salt and pepper to taste [or use garlic salt]
Pinch cayenne pepper
Paprika

Directions
Preheat oven to 350° F.

Grease 2 qt. casserole dish.

In a large skillet saute onion and pepper in butter.

Add cream cheese and whipping cream; reduce heat and heat till melted.

Add tuna, green beans, pimientos and seasonings.

Transfer to casserole dish; add shredded cheese.

Top with Parmesan cheese and sprinkle with paprika.

Bake 30 minutes or until cheeses melted and lightly browned.

Let stand 5 minutes before serving.

Makes 8 servings

Baked Spinach Casserole

This one is an ideal vegetarian meal but it also makes an excellent side dish if you so choose. This is also a good option if need a dish to pass that will be diet friendly.

Ingredients

3 - 10 oz packages frozen chopped spinach -- thawed and drained
3 - 4 oz cans of mushroom slices -- drained
4 whole large eggs
2 cups eggbeaters
3/4 cup low fat yogurt
3/4 cup grated Parmesan cheese
2 cups Hunt's Tomato Sauce
16 oz shredded mozzarella
1 teaspoon garlic salt
1/4 teaspoon black pepper
3 teaspoon basil

Directions

Preheat oven to 350° F. Spray a 12x16 baking pan with cooking spray.

Beat eggs with a fork then stir in all the spices, the yogurt and the Parmesan cheese. Mix well then stir in the spinach and mushrooms. Spoon into the prepared pan and tap to settle into an even layer.

Bake, uncovered, for 40 minutes then spread the sauce on top and sprinkle on the cheese. Bake an additional 15 minutes.

Let sit 15 minutes before cutting the casserole!

Yields: 8 big servings

Low Carb Egg And Cottage Cheese Salad

Protein day leave out salad / Meal day with salad

An easy low fat and low carb egg salad with no mayo at all!

35 Minutes to Prepare and Cook

Ingredients

2 hard boiled eggs (one yolk can be removed)
1/3 cup 1% cottage cheese
Salt (seasoned salt is best flavor with egg)
Pepper
(Add a little dill, Dijon mustard or other favorite to give this a little more flavor.)

Directions

Hard boil eggs and remove one of the yolks to lower the fat.

Chop egg whites and one yolk. Mix in cottage cheese, and season to taste.

You will have a high protein low fat egg salad in no time.

Makes 1 serving

Spinach, Leek and Feta Quiche

Ingredients

1 large Leek
1 10 oz package of Chopped Spinach (frozen)
3 Large Eggs
3 large Egg Whites
8 oz package 1/3 Less Fat Philadelphia Cream Cheese
6 ounces Plain Low fat Yogurt
4 oz Feta Cheese
1/4 cup Parmesan Cheese
Cooking Spray

Directions

Start by spraying a cake pan with PAM spray to have ready for the quiche and set the oven to 350° F.

Cook leeks in cooking spray over medium heat until soft. Squeeze liquid out of spinach and add to leeks. In food processor or in bowl with electric mixer, process cream cheese. Add yogurt; process. Add eggs one at a time, while processing, until smooth. Stir in feta cheese and Parmesan cheese. Pour mixture over vegetables; stir to combine well. Now pour the mixture in to your oiled pan.

Bake in 350° F oven 50 minutes, or until set. Allow to stand 10 minutes before cutting.

Makes 6 slices

Cream of Broccoli and Cauliflower Soup

40 Minutes to Prepare and Cook

Ingredients

1 lb. mixture of broccoli and cauliflower coarsely chopped (about 2 cups)
6 scallions (green onions), chopped
2 cups Vegetable Broth
1 garlic clove, minced
1 cup nonfat evaporated milk
40 grams vegetable protein powder (optional**)
2 tablespoon Smart Balance 37% Light Buttery Spread
1 teaspoon dried Marjoram
1 teaspoon black pepper

Directions

Combine broth, broccoli/cauliflower mixture (save about 1/3 cup of broccoli for later), garlic, and scallions in a saucepan. Bring to a boil. Reduce heat and simmer covered for about 10 minutes until veggies are tender.

Remove from heat and cool for a few minutes. Transfer to a blender or food processor and puree until smooth.

Steam the remaining 1/3 cup of broccoli in the microwave. Finely chop.

In the saucepan, melt the margarine. Mix in marjoram and pepper. Gradually stir in milk until smooth. Cook over medium heat, stirring, until thick and bubbling. Add the pureed soup and broccoli to milk mixture and heat to serving temperature. Salt and pepper to taste.

Makes 4 servings

Lentil Soup

An easy dish to make on the weekend and have plenty of for the week. It makes an easy lunch to take to work. To up the protein you can also serve it with grilled chicken.

2 hours to Prepare and Cook

Ingredients

1 bunch fresh cilantro
12 cloves of garlic
1/4 cup & 3 Tablespoon olive oil
2 & 1/2 teaspoons of salt divided
2 large onions, chopped fine
1 lb. of lentils, washed and drained
1 1/2 teaspoons cinnamon
12 cups of water
1 (10 ounce) box of frozen spinach
2 medium potatoes, cubed
6 tablespoons lemon juice

Directions

In a small food processor place garlic, 3 Tablespoon olive oil, and 1/2 teaspoon of salt and process the mixture until it forms a paste. Set aside.

In a large nonstick cast iron pot, saute onions in 1/4 cup of olive oil until light brown.

Add lentils and mix allow to cook on medium heat for a few minutes to allow the flavors to mix. Add cinnamon and water.

Turn heat to medium-high and cook uncovered for 45 minutes, stirring occasionally.

Turn heat to medium, add remaining salt, spinach, potatoes and cilantro paste. Cook uncovered, on low heat until lentils are creamy.

Add lemon juice and allow to cook for 10 minutes.

Soup can be served warm or cold.

Number of Servings: 8-10

Spinach and Feta Garlic Rolls

Ingredients

Dough:

- 2 cups carbalose flour
- 1/3 cup vital wheat gluten
- 1/2 teaspoon salt
- 1/2 cup whole milk, lukewarm (about 110F)
- 1/2 cup water, lukewarm (abut 110F)
- 1 package rapid rise yeast
- 1 large egg, lightly beaten

Filling:

- 1 12 oz package frozen spinach, thawed and squeezed of excess moisture
- 1 cup crumbled feta cheese
- 1/2 teaspoon marjoram
- 1/2 teaspoon salt
- 1/2 teaspoon freshly ground pepper

Garlic Butter:

- 2 tablespoon butter, softened
- 2 cloves garlic, pressed

Directions

Preheat oven to 200° F for 10 minutes and then turn oven off.

In a medium bowl, stir together carbalose flour, gluten flour and salt. Set aside In the bowl of your mixer, combine milk and water. Sprinkle yeast over and mix well. Mix in egg until combined.

With the mixer on low speed, slowly add flour mixture until combined. Dough may be quite sticky, but do not add any more flour.

With greased hands, shape dough into a smooth ball and place in a lightly greased bowl. Cover tightly with plastic wrap. Place in warm oven for 30-45 minutes, or until doubled in size.

Meanwhile, combine spinach, feta, marjoram, salt and pepper together in a medium bowl.

Roll out dough on a lightly greased surface into a rough rectangle, 12 x 16 inches or so. Spread spinach mixture over dough, leaving a 1/2 inch border around all edges. Starting at a longer side, roll up dough tightly into a log and pinch to seal the edge.

Cut log with a serrated knife into 16 equal portions and place on a parchment-lined baking sheet. Put back into warm oven and let rise until doubled, about 20 to 30 more minutes. Remove from oven and increase heat to 375° F.

In a small bowl, combine butter and garlic and brush over the top of each roll. Once oven is preheated, bake rolls 18-20 minutes or until golden brown.

Serve warm..

Makes 16 servings

Vegetarian Ramen Noodle Soup

I would recommend adding Tofu to it if you wish to keep it vegetarian or serving with grilled chicken to add your protein to the dish.

Ingredients:
1 onion, thinly sliced
2 tablespoons canola oil
7 cups vegetable broth
3 tablespoons soy sauce
1 Package Shirataki Noodles (Miracle Noodles, I get mine on Amazon)
1/2 to 1 teaspoon Chinese chili oil or sesame chili oil
1 teaspoon finely chopped ginger root
Salt, to taste
Green onions, thinly sliced, for garnishing

Directions:
Heat the canola oil in a large pot over medium heat. Add the onions and ginger and cook until the onions become soft, about 3-5 minutes. Add the vegetable broth and raise the heat to high.

Meanwhile, drain the Shirataki Noodles. Rinse the noodles for at least 2 to 3 minutes under warm running water.

When the vegetable broth comes to a roiling boil, add the soy sauce and the sesame chili oil or the Chinese chili oil. Add salt, to taste. Finally, add the noodles and continue cooking about 5 minutes. Serve in bowls and garnish with the green onions.

Tofu Lo-Mein

Not a tofu fan? You can easily substitute chicken or shrimp for the tofu. Serves 2.

Ingredients

1 (16 ounce) package extra firm tofu
2 tablespoons olive oil
2 Packages Shirataki Noodles (Miracle Noodles, I get mine on Amazon)
2 tablespoons onion powder
2 tablespoons ground ginger
2 tablespoons garlic powder
2 tablespoons ground black pepper
Salt, to taste
1 (16 ounce) package frozen stir-fry vegetables
1 1/2 cups water
1 tablespoon soy sauce, or to taste

Directions

Press tofu between paper towels to remove some of the water; cut in to bite size cubes. Heat olive oil in large skillet over medium-high heat. Add tofu, and fry until golden brown, about 15 minutes. Stir occasionally to prevent burning.

Meanwhile bring water to a boil in a medium saucepan. First, and terribly important, is that you must drain the Shirataki Noodles. Rinse the noodles for at least 2 to 3 minutes under warm running water. Add noodles to boiling water and boil for about 2 -3 minutes. Drain well.

Add the stir-fry vegetables to the pan with the tofu, and onion powder, garlic powder, black pepper and salt. Cook, stirring occasionally until vegetables are tender, but not mushy. Add noodles, and stir to blend. Season with soy sauce to taste and serve.

Portobello Burgers

(protein/vegetable meal)

Ingredients

4 sun-dried tomatoes
Boiling water
4 portobello mushrooms
1/4 cup Gorgonzola cheese
1 tablespoon plus 1 teaspoon extra virgin olive oil
and pepper to taste

Directions

Take the sun dried tomatoes and soak in boiling water for 10 minutes. Remove them from the water allow to dry on paper towel and finely slice them.

Preheat a rill pan to medium-high heat.

Remove the stems from the mushroom caps them slice it in half so you make two bun halves. One one half top with approximately 1 tablespoon of cheese and 1 tablespoon of tomato. Place the other bun on top and then brush the outsides of the mushroom with olive oil.

Place the burger in the grill pan and cook for 2 minutes per side. Season with salt and pepper if desired.

Makes 4 servings

7

Desserts

Favorite Ice Cream Base

This is the my go-to ice cream recipe. I use it to make most of my flavors. One of my favorites follows this one but my second favorite and it's close is to add 2 Peach Health Flavor Mix ins.

Ingredients
1 cup heavy cream
1 cup half and half
2 Eggs
3/4 cup Splenda
2 teaspoon vanilla
2 Scoops Sweet Cream Protein Powder

Directions
Pour all of the ingredients into a blender and mix well

Add mix to ice cream maker and follow manufacturers instructions.

It's better than any store bought ice cream

Chocolate Ice Cream

Ingredients

1 cup heavy cream
1 cup half and half
2 Eggs
3/4 cup Splenda
2 teaspoon vanilla
2 Scoops Sweet Cream Protein Powder
2 Teaspoon cocoa

Directions

Pour all of the ingredients into a blender and mix well

Add mix to ice cream maker and follow manufacturers instructions.

Almond Vanilla Ice Cream

Ingredients

1 ½ cup water
½ cup almonds, raw and unsalted
2 cups heavy cream
2 scoops Sweet Cream Protein
2 eggs
1 teaspoon pure vanilla
Liquid Stevia(to taste…start with 1/8 teaspoon)

Directions

Mix water and almonds in blender until it makes almond milk.

Add other ingredients and blend on low until eggs are mixed in.

Pour in Ice Cream Maker and follow instruction manual. Enjoy!

Makes 8 servings

Italian Cream Pudding

You haven't lived until you've tried this pudding! Smooth, rich, and delectable!! Impress your family and friends with this one!

Ingredients

1 package unflavored gelatin
1 1/2 cup half and half
1/2 teaspoon vanilla
2 cup cottage cheese
4 Teaspoon sf strawberry preserves
1/2 cup Splenda

Directions

Sprinkle gelatin over 1/2 cup half-and-half in medium saucepan; let stand 5 minutes to soften.

Stir in remaining 1 cup half-and-half, Splenda, and vanilla

Cook on low heat until gelatin is dissolved..Stir frequently..DO NOT BOIL!

Pour cream mixture in blender; add cottage cheese and blend until pureed..

Pour into 8 custard cups or souffle dishes. Refrigerate until set.
Sugar-Free strawberry preserves are optional, but add a lot to the dish.

Notes
*Optional: After the pudding has set, microwave strawberry preserves for 15 seconds..Spoon 1/2 teaspoon over each dessert..Serve immediately and enjoy!

Low Carb Protein Brownies

These low carb, low calorie brownies will have you fooled.

Minutes to Prepare: 10

Minutes to Cook: 20

Ingredients

1 Tablespoon. Oil
1 Stick Butter
1 1/2 Cup. Splenda
1 teaspoon. Vanilla Extract
2 Eggs
1/3 Cup. Cocoa
1/2 Cup. Sweet Cream Protein Powder
1/4 teaspoon baking powder
1/8 teaspoon salt
1/4 Cup. Milk

Directions

Heat oven to 350° F. Grease 8"x8" pan.

Melt Butter. Add Splenda and vanilla. Add eggs and beat with a spoon.

Add cocoa, protein powder, baking powder and salt. Mix well. Add oil and milk. Mix well. Put in baking dish.

Bake 20 or until toothpick comes out clean.

Makes 9 servings

Protein Pudding

Ingredients

1 box fat-free, sugar-free chocolate or vanilla pudding
2 cups skim milk
2 scoops Sweet Cream Protein Powder

Directions

Mix all ingredients in a blender for 45 seconds

Pour into four small bowls.

Allow pudding to set for an hour.

May top with suger free cool whip and enjoy.

Makes 4 servings

Baked Custard

Ingredients

1 whole egg
1 egg yolk
1/2 cup heavy cream (whipping cream)
1/2 cup water
1 1/2 tbsp. Splenda
1 1/2 tsp vanilla extract
1/8 tsp salt
Ground nutmeg

Directions

Preheat oven to 350° F.

Lightly beat the egg and yolk with a whisk.

Add cream, water, Splenda, vanilla and salt and mix well.

Pour into two ungreased 6 ounce custard cups.

Sprinkle with nutmeg.

Set in a pan containing 1/2 to 1 inch of hot water and bake for 35 minutes or until set.

Makes 2 servings

Chocolate Peanut Butter Cups

Ingredients
1 sugar free fudge pop
2 tablespoons natural-style peanut butter
2 teaspoons sugar free whipped topping

Directions
On a small plat or bowl microwave fudge pop for about 10 seconds until soft.

Scrape fudge pop off of stick into bowl.

Add peanut butter and whipped topping and mix well together.

Place bowl back in the freezer for 15-20 minutes to allow to set back up and enjoy.

Peanut Butter Cheesecake Cupcakes

Ingredients
8 oz. low fat Cream Cheese, softened
1 large Egg
1 1/2 Tablespoons Vanilla Extract
4 packets Splenda
4 Tablespoons All Natural Peanut Butter

Directions
Preheat oven to 350° F.

Mix together all ingredients and blend for about 5 minutes.

Line muffin pan with paper muffin cups and then fill each 3/4 of the way with mixture

Bake for 20 minutes. Allow to cool before serving.

Cream Cheese Gelatin Cups

Ingredients

2 ounces low fat cream cheese
2 tbsp. heavy cream
2-3 tbsp. Splenda (use to taste)
1 packet of prepared sugar-free jello divided in 4 cups - Cherry or Strawberry work well in this recipe

Directions

Warm the cream cheese for 30 seconds in the microwave.

Whip together the cream cheese and Splenda.

Top each cup of jello with 1/4 of the mixture.

Let it set for a couple of minutes.

Lime Fluff Dessert

Ingredients
1 15-16 oz. tub of low fat cottage cheese
1 tub of sugar free cool whip (thawed)
1 package sugar free Lime Jello
1 can crushed pineapple – Drained well (optional if during extreme burn)

Directions
Mix the cottage cheese with the lime jello

If using pineapple be sure to drain this super well. I like to even line a colander with paper towel and press it to get the excess liquid out. After it is as dry as you can get it mix in the pineapple with the cottage cheese / jello mixture

Mix in the Cool Whip

Place in the fridge to allow it to setup preferably over night.

Enjoy!

Makes 12 servings

Cinnamon Bun Protein Cake

Submitted by Tina Gay

Ingredients

6 packs Stevia
3 scoops Vi-Shape Mix
1.5 cup ground oats
1 tablespoon Baking Powder
1/4 teaspoon Sea Salt
2 teaspoon Cinnamon
2 eggs
1 cup almond milk
3 tablespoon plain greek yogurt

Topping:
2 teaspoon cinnamon
1 teaspoon powdered stevia

Directions

Preheat oven to 350.

Don't get all fancy, just mix all ingredients together in a large mixing bowl and whisk together!

Mix the extra 2 teaspoon of cinnamon and the 1 teaspoon of Stevia together and sprinkle over top when done baking

Bake for 25-30 minutes

Low Carb Quick Chocolate Almond Ice Cream

This is a fake out ice cream but works well if you are without an ice cream maker and looking for a sweet treat or just want an alternative.

Ingredients

2 tablespoons sliced almonds
1 cup heavy cream
1/2 cup sugar substitute (recommended: Splenda)
1 teaspoon no sugar added vanilla extract
1/8 teaspoon no sugar added almond extract
1 tablespoon unsweetened cocoa powder
2 tablespoons whole milk ricotta cheese

Directions

Preheat oven to 350° F.

Spread almonds out on a sheet pan and bake for about 5 to 7 minutes until just golden brown. (Watch them carefully as they can burn easily.) Remove and cool.

With an electric mixer on high, whip the heavy cream in a bowl just until frothy and add in the sugar substitute, extracts, cocoa powder, and ricotta cheese. Continue to whip on high until peaks form. Be careful not to over-whip, or cream will break. Fold in toasted almonds.

Using a 3-ounce ice cream scoop, place 1 scoop each in a champagne glass and freeze as "faux" ice cream or serve refrigerated as a parfait.

If desired, garnish with low carb whipped cream, toasted almonds, a strawberry fan, cocoa powder, and a sprig of fresh mint.

Meringue cookies

Ingredients

1 scoop of Vanilla egg white protein powder (sometimes you can find these in single serving packets)
3 egg whites
1/2 capful of vanilla
Pinch of cream of tartar
1 package. Stevia or your favorite sweetener

Directions

Preheat oven to 325° F

Beat egg white, stevia and cream of tartar till stiff.

Add vanilla and egg white powder and beat again till stiff. Drop on cookie sheet by the teaspoonfuls

Bake for 10-12 min until toasty brown all over. Watch closely as these brown quickly. Let set for 20 mins or so to cool.

Strawberry Cream Cheese Pie

Ingredients

1 8 oz. box cream cheese
1-2 packets of Stevia(depends on your sweet taste)
1/2 teaspoon vanilla
1 small box of sugar free strawberry gelatin
Strawberry preserves (Sugar free)

Directions

Blend cream cheese, Stevia and vanilla in bowl.

Whip till well blended. Pour in 8 in. size pie pan or glass dish. This will be your crust.

Make jello accordingly to box instructions.

Pour prepared jello over crust. Place in fridge for 1 hr. or more till firmly set.

Before serving spread preserves over top.

Serve with suger free cool whip.

Makes 8 servings

Low Carb Cream Cheese Clouds

Ingredients
1/2 teaspoon pure vanilla
2 tablespoon unsweetened cocoa powder
2 Teaspoon Splenda
1 Teaspoon butter, melted
8 oz original cream cheese (room temp)

Directions
Mix vanilla, cocoa, splenda and butter in a bowl.

Add cream cheese, room temp stir till combined.

Take a teaspoon and dollop 1 at a time on foil, wax paper or cookie tray.

Freeze and then bag. Eat frozen or wait till it unfreezes a bit.

Makes 9 servings

Peanut Butter Mound Cupcakes

Recipe Submitted by Flo Woodring

Ingredients

1 cup. Vi-Shape Protein powder
1/2 cup. Almond Milk
6 oz Plain Greek yogurt
1 teaspoon Baking soda
1/4 cup. Powdered Peanut Butter, heaping
All Natural Peanut Butter or Almond Butter

Directions

Preheat oven to 350° F

Mix all ingredients together.

Fill sprayed cupcake tins about 1/2-3/4 with batter.

Take a mound of Natural Peanut Butter and put it on top of the batter and press it in a tad.

Bake for 20-25 minutes.

Chocolate Mini Muffins

Recipe Submitted by Libby Watford

Ingredients

2 Cups Vi-Shape protein powder
1 Cup Milk
2 teaspoon. Baking Powder
1/2 Cup Cocoa
1/2 Cup Splenda
2 Eggs
1 Cup Olive Oil Mayonnaise

Directions

Bake at 350 for about 12 Minutes.

Makes about 2-3 dozen mini cupcakes. Top with Sugar Free Cool Whip.

Makes 12 servings

8

Page Cycle Plan & Sample Menus

So many of you have emailed me that they have struggled with what to eat. I didn't want to put you in a box and tell you that you had to eat a specific food at a specific time because I wanted to be sure you enjoyed what you are eating. However, for those of you that want those specific this is for you. I am including the Page Cycle Diet charts here again followed by a sample menu with recipes in this book to give you an idea of what to eat. Keep in mind if you don't like the food that is listed swap it out for another recipe that will fit the cycle.

PAGE CYCLE
break the cycle

Sample Menu: Extreme Burn Cycle

Use this calendar to manage your success! The Extreme Burn Cycle is the starting cycle of the Page Cycle that reprograms how your body responds to food. The emphasis is eating protein-only for 4 days and adding back in smart carbs of veggies and fruit early in the day, for 3 days to create contrast within the body. Recommended for the first 2-weeks to maximize results. The Extreme Burn Cycle can also be repeated, following the Burn or Steady Burn cycles, anytime you need to get back on track to your goal.

☐ Protein-Only Day   P = Protein
■ Protein/"Smart Meal" Day

	1 Monday	2 Tuesday	3 Wednesday	4 Thursday	5 Friday	6 Saturday	7 Sunday
Breakfast	Protein Shake	Protein Shake	Mock Oatmeal	Protein Shake	Protein Shake	Protein Pancakes	Baked Egg Muffins
Snack	Cheesy Edamame	2-4 oz. Plain Green Yogurt w/ Chopped Pecans or Walnuts	Protein Shake	2-4 oz. Low-fat Cottage Cheese	Edamame "Hummus" w/ Celery	Mug Muffin	Protein Shake
Lunch	Protein Shake	Protein Shake	Herb Grilled Chicken w/ Caprese Salad	Protein Shake	Caesar Salad with Lemon Pepper Shrimp	Protein Shake	Low Carb Egg And Cottage Cheese Salad
Snack	2-4 oz Cubed Cheddar Cheese & Turkey	Tuna & Celery	Protein Shake	Pinwheels	Protein Shake	Buffalo Chicken Dip w/ Celery	Protein Shake
Dinner	Taco Bake	Crock Pot Pizza Chicken	Meat Muffins	Tofu Lo-Mein	Low Carb Tuna Casserole	Sloppy Joe Stuffed Peppers	Fake Out Lasagna

My Notes: **Fill in below:**

My daily protein amount is (minimum 1/2 your body weight in grams):	
My daily water intake is (1/2 body weight in ounces):	

Supplements will increase your chances of success see www.pagecyclediet.com for more info.

PAGE CYCLE
break the cycle

Extreme Burn Cycle

Use this calendar to manage your success! The Extreme Burn Cycle is the starting cycle of the Page Cycle that reprograms how your body responds to food. The emphasis is eating protein-only for 4 days and adding back in smart carbs of veggies and fruit early in the day, for 3 days to create contrast within the body. Recommended for the first 2-weeks to maximize results. The Extreme Burn Cycle can also be repeated, following the Burn or Steady Burn cycles, anytime you need to get back on track to your goal.

☐ Protein-Only Day P = Protein
■ Protein/"Smart Meal" Day

1	2	3	4	5	6	7
Breakfast							

	1	2	3	4	5	6	7
Breakfast	P	P	P	P	P	P	P
Snack	P	P	P	P	P	P	P
Lunch	P	P	"Smart Meal"	P	"Smart Meal"	P	"Smart Meal"
Snack	P	P	P	P	P	P	P
Dinner	P	P	P	P	P	P	P

My Notes:	**Fill in below:**
My daily protein amount is (minimum 1/2 your body weight in grams):	
My daily water intake is (1/2 body weight in ounces):	

Smart Protein/Fat Choices:

Chicken, turkey, beef, roast beef, steak, omelets, jerky, salmon, tuna, halibut, tilapia, cod, shrimp, scallops, lobster, crab, oysters, tofu, eggs, Canadian bacon, string cheese, cottage cheese, mozzarella cheese, Laughing Cow Swiss cheese, Kroger Carbmaster yogurt (higher protein than carbs), avocado, nuts and seeds, olives, olive oil, sunflower seed butter, buffalo, flax seed oil, almond butter

Smart Carb Choices:

Brown rice, wild rice, whole grain rice, veggie pasta, egg noodles, whole grain pasta, whole grain bread, whole grain bagel, oatmeal, fiber cereal, whole grain tortillas, whole grain pita bread, rice cakes, boiled oatmeal, legumes/beans (any kind)

On black days, have a "Smart Meal" for lunch (A "Smart Meal" is a 500-600 calorie meal with Protein, Vegetables, Smart Carbs and Fruit if you wish). Then have protein the rest of the day.

Supplements will increase your chances of success see www.pagecyclediet.com for more info.

Smart Fruit and Vegetable Choices:

Sweet potatoes, zucchini, asparagus, broccoli, brussel sprouts, spinach, mushrooms, onions, romaine/iceberg lettuce, red/green/yellow bell peppers, celery, cauliflower, tomatoes, cucumbers, green beans, onions, artichoke, cabbage, pickles, hot peppers, leeks, rhubarb, V-8, apples, oranges, peaches, tangerines, grapes, grapefruit, cantaloupe, pears, all berries, pineapple, plums, mango, watermelon

My Shopping List:

PAGE CYCLE
break the cycle

Burn Cycle

The mid-point cycle of the Page Cycle. You will repeat the Burn Cycle for majority of the time until you achieve your goal weight. The Burn Cycle supports further reduction with four days of protein and unlimited vegetables, and three days of adding back in smart carbohydrates from whole grains, and pairing a fruit with a protein for a healthy snack once daily. Fruit and grain should be eaten early in the day. Choose to reward yourself with one guilt free meal, but suggest eating protein-only the following day.

All Protein Day (white)	P = Protein
Protein/Vegetable Day (black)	V = Vegetable
Protein/Vegetable/Grain Day (grey)	F = Fruit
Optional Guilt Free Meal (1 per week; you choose day)	G = Grain

1		2	3	4	5	6	7
Breakfast	P	P, V	P, V	P, V	P, V	P, V	P, V
Snack	P	P	P, F	P	P, F	P	P, F
Lunch	P	P, V, F	P, V, G	P, V, F	P, V, G	P, V, F	P, V, G
Snack	P	P, V	P, V	P, V	P, V	P, V	P, V
Dinner	P	P, V	P, V	P, V	P, V	P, V	P, V

My Notes:	Fill in below:
My daily protein amount is (minimum 1/2 your body weight in grams):	
My daily water intake is (1/2 body weight in ounces):	

On black days, eat fruit and vegetable by lunch time. Have protein the rest of the day.

Supplements will increase your chances of success see www.pagecyclediet.com for more info.

Smart Protein/Fat Choices:

Chicken, turkey, beef, roast beef, steak, omelets, jerky, salmon, tuna, halibut, tilapia, cod, shrimp, scallops, lobster, crab, oysters, tofu, eggs, Canadian bacon, string cheese, cottage cheese, mozzarella cheese, Laughing Cow Swiss cheese, Kroger Carbmaster yogurt (higher protein than carbs), avocado, nuts and seeds, olives, olive oil, sunflower seed butter, buffalo, flax seed oil, almond butter

Smart Carb Choices:

Brown rice, wild rice, whole grain rice, veggie pasta, egg noodles, whole grain pasta, whole grain bread, whole grain bagel, oatmeal, fiber cereal, whole grain tortillas, whole grain pita bread, rice cakes, boiled oatmeal, legumes/beans (any kind)

Smart Fruit and Vegetable Choices:

Sweet potatoes, zucchini, asparagus, broccoli, brussel sprouts, spinach, mushrooms, onions, romaine/iceberg lettuce, red/green/yellow bell peppers, celery, cauliflower, tomatoes, cucumbers, green beans, onions, artichoke, cabbage, pickles, hot peppers, leeks, rhubarb, V-8, apples, oranges, peaches, tangerines, grapes, grapefruit, cantaloupe, pears, all berries, pineapple, plums, mango, watermelon

My Shopping List:

Steady Burn Cycle

The Steady Burn Cycle helps you maintain your goal weight as part of a healthy lifestyle. Eating smart proteins with smart carbohydrates is now habit. The Steady Burn Cycle empowers you with more flexibility of how you choose to eat to sustain your goal weight. Fruit and grain should be eaten before 4 pm. Opt to reward yourself with one guilt free meal during the week, but suggest eating all protein the following day.

All Protein Day	P = Protein
Protein/Vegetable Day	V = Vegetable
Protein/Vegetable/Grain Day	F = Fruit
Optional Guilt Free Meal	G = Grain

	1	2	3	4	5	6	7
Breakfast	P	P, V	P, V	P, V	P, V	P, V	P, V
Snack	P	P	P, F	P, F	P	P, F	P, F
Lunch	P	P, V, F	P, V, G	P, V, G	P, V, F	P, V, G	P, V, G
Snack	P	P, V	P, V	P, V	P, V	P, V	P, V
Dinner	P	P, V	P, V	P, V	P, V	P, V	P, V

My Notes: Fill in below:

My daily protein amount is (minimum 1/2 your body weight in grams):	
My daily water intake is (1/2 body weight in ounces):	

On black days, eat fruit and vegetable by lunch time. Have protein the rest of the day.

Supplements will increase your chances of success see www.pagecyclediet.com for more info.

Smart Protein/Fat Choices:

Chicken, turkey, beef, roast beef, steak, omelets, jerky, salmon, tuna, halibut, tilapia, cod, shrimp, scallops, lobster, crab, oysters, tofu, eggs, Canadian bacon, string cheese, cottage cheese, mozzarella cheese, Laughing Cow Swiss cheese, Kroger Carbmaster yogurt (higher protein than carbs), avocado, nuts and seeds, olives, olive oil, sunflower seed butter, buffalo, flax seed oil, almond butter

Smart Carb Choices:

Brown rice, wild rice, whole grain rice, veggie pasta, egg noodles, whole grain pasta, whole grain bread, whole grain bagel, oatmeal, fiber cereal, whole grain tortillas, whole grain pita bread, rice cakes, boiled oatmeal, legumes/beans (any kind)

Smart Fruit and Vegetable Choices:

Sweet potatoes, zucchini, asparagus, broccoli, brussel sprouts, spinach, mushrooms, onions, romaine/iceberg lettuce, red/green/yellow bell peppers, celery, cauliflower, tomatoes, cucumbers, green beans, onions, artichoke, cabbage, pickles, hot peppers, leeks, rhubarb, V-8, apples, oranges, peaches, tangerines, grapes, grapefruit, cantaloupe, pears, all berries, pineapple, plums, mango, watermelon

My Shopping List:

Page Cycle Diet Recipe Chart

	Extreme Burn	Smart Meal / Burn
Protein Pancakes - Jen's Way—8	●	
Crustless Spinach Mini Quiches—9	●	
Smoked Salmon Scramble—10	●	
Caramel Latte Blended Ice Coffee Shake—11	●	
Breakfast Pudding—12	●	
Cinnamon Muffins —13	●	
Mock Oatmeal—14	●	
On The Go Breakfast Cookies—15	●	
Baked Egg Muffins—16	●	
Cinnamon Rolls—17	●	
Chocolate Donuts with Peanut Butter Glaze—19	●	
Almond Flour French Toast—21	●	
Almond Flour Bread—22	●	
Blackberry Lemon Ricotta Parfaits—23		●
Crepes—24	●	
Sausage Egg Bake—25	●	
Scotch Eggs—26	●	
Cottage Cheese, Black Bean and Avocado Salsa—28		●
Protein Microwave Brownie—29	●	
Low Carb Herb & Cheese Crackers—30	●	
Pinwheels—31	●	
Deviled Eggs—32	●	
Ham-Wrapped Egg with Tuna—33	●	
Mug Muffin—34	●	
Tuna & Celery—35	●	

	Extreme Burn	Smart Meal / Burn
Buffalo Chicken Dip—36	●	
Low Carb Cheesy Crackers—37	●	
Kale Chips—38		●
Cheesy Edamame—39	●	
Edamame "Hummus"—40	●	
Parmesan Cauliflower—42		●
Cauliflower Hash Browns—43		●
Zucchini And Mushroom "Noodles"—44		●
Cauliflower "Potato" Salad—45		●
Green Beans with Almond Slivers—47		●
Parmesan Grilled Asparagus—48		●
Grilled Romaine Salad—49		●
Cucumber Salad—50		●
Stuffed Mushrooms—51		●
Caesar Salad—52		●
Lemon-Nut Kale—53		●
Balsamic Broccoli—54		●
Caprese Salad—55		●
Quick 'N Easy Balsamic Chicken —58	●	
Easy Turkey Chili—59	●	
Crock Pot Pizza Chicken—60	●	
Herb Grilled Chicken—61	●	
Mexican Chicken—62	●	
Enchilada Chicken—63	●	
Dijon Chicken —64	●	
Spicy Chicken & Spinach Casserole—65	●	
Chicken Basil Meatloaf—66	●	

	Extreme Burn	Smart Meal / Burn
Asparagus, Tomato, Chicken and Penne Pasta—67		●
Awesome Southwest Tortilla Soup—68		●
Bruschetta Quinoa—69		●
Asian Chicken and Macaroni Salad—71		●
Meat Muffins—72	●	
Low Carb, High Protein Taco Bake—73	●	
Turkey Soufflé—75		
Crock Pot Beef And Peppers—76	●	
Crock Pot Meatballs—77	●	
Sloppy Joe Stuffed Peppers —79	●	
Chili Taco Salad—80		●
Fake Out Lasagna—81		●
Crustless Pizza—83	●	
Mini Spinach Meatloaf—84	●	
Crock Pot Soy Sauce Ribs—85	●	
Crock Pot Carnitas—86	●	
Grilled Salmon—87	●	
Salmon Salad—88		●
Slammin' Salmon—89	●	
Tuna Patty Melt—90	●	
Lemon Pepper Shrimp—91	●	
Shrimp Lettuce Wraps—92		●
Low Carb Tuna Casserole—93	●	
Baked Spinach Casserole—95		●
Low Carb Egg And Cottage Cheese Salad—96	●	
Spinach, Leek and Feta Quiche—97		●
Cream of Broccoli and Cauliflower Soup —98		●

	Extreme Burn	Smart Meal / Burn
Lentil Soup—99		●
Spinach and Feta Garlic Rolls—101		●
Vegetarian Ramen Noodle Soup—103	●	
Tofu Lo-Mein—104	●	
Portobello Burgers —105	●	
Favorite Ice Cream Base—108	●	
Chocolate Ice Cream—109	●	
Almond Vanilla Ice Cream—110	●	
Italian Cream Pudding—111	●	
Low Carb Protein Brownies—112	●	
Protein Pudding—113	●	
Baked Custard—114	●	
Chocolate Peanut Butter Cups—115	●	
Peanut Butter Cheesecake Cupcakes—116	●	
Cream Cheese Gelatin Cups—117	●	
Lime Fluff Dessert—118	●	
Cinnamon Bun Protein Cake —119	●	
Low Carb Quick Chocolate Almond Ice Cream—120	●	
Meringue cookies—121	●	
Strawberry Cream Cheese Pie—122	●	
Low Carb Cream Cheese Clouds—123	●	
Peanut Butter Mound Cupcakes—124	●	
Chocolate Mini Muffins—125	●	

9

Final Thoughts

I want you to know that I'm in this with you. I have so enjoyed hearing from so many of you how The Page Cycle Diet has changed their lives. Your success stores make my day. So many of you even contributed their favorite recipes to this book! Please keep them coming, if you have a favorite recipe that you come up with inspired by this book be sure to share it, send an email to cookbook@pagecyclediet.com

Nothing would make me happier than to hear about your success, so e-mail me at success@pagecyclediet.com. When I developed the Page Cycle Diet four years ago, my goal was to empower ten million people to lose 100 million pounds. I think we are well on our way to making that goat. As always, I will continue to provide education and support to anyone who is following my plan. Please visit my website www.pagecyclediet.com often as I will continue to improve the support I provide or to get more information on supplements I recommend.

I know the Page Cycle Diet works. Not just for some people, but for everybody. The only variable in this equation is you. I believe in you and I know that you can reach your goal.

Page Cycle Diet Success Stories

"For many years I have fought my weight, using some amazing Meal Replacement supplements I had lost 50 lbs but needed a boost to keep going, after starting on the PageCycleDiet in just 4 days I had lost an amazing 10lbs more and feel great!"

Dale Peake

"Over the past few months I have had the opportunity to use a fantastic meal replacement that has netted me some great results.

In my first 90 days of taking this meal replacement I lost over 23 pounds.

These were great results but I felt like by body hit a wall and I needed something more to help continue my weight loss.

A great friend of mine suggested that you and I get in touch and that first call with you produced the information I was looking for to step up my weight loss journey.

In my first 48 hours I'm down 4 pounds and 5.4 lbs after 72 hours. The support you have provided for me has been Awesome!!!

The strategies you provide in your book was exactly what not only myself but millions of people are looking for. I'm going to be fifty this year and I'm committed to getting in the best shape of my life!!!

Thanks for you support"

Ryan Vanderpool

"Day 1 successful and incredibly easy to follow. Can't believe how much I ate yesterday. Worked out last night and feeling like a million bucks today. But seriously, -4.6 lbs overnight??!!??

I got off the scale and got back on again just to be sure I wasn't sleep drunk and reading it wrong. Woohoo !!! I'm bringing my sexy back !!"

Shelley Vervaecke

"SOOOO stoked!!! Down 9 LBS in 8 Days!!! 3 1/2 inches off my waist and I LOVE IT!!! Gettin my sexy back!! Watch out beach!!! Gonna be one hot mama headin your way!!"

Raylene Lynas

"WAHOOOOO!!! I stepped on the scale after 10 days!! I am down 9.5 lbs. :) I love the Page Cycle Diet!!"

Shawn Nistler- Heinen

Page Cycle Diet Daily Journal Page

Date:	Day of 90
Grams of protein:	
Ounces of water:	
Weight :	
Notes for the day: Emotional notes, etc.	

Index

D

E

F

G

H

I

K

L

M

N

O

P

Z

Acknowledgements

From Mike:

First off I want to thank the many people who have read The Page Cycle Diet Book and implemented it into their lives to make lasting change in how they feel.

I want to thank Jennifer Du Charme, without her this project never would have happened. She had the inspiration for this book and took the lead making it happen. Jennifer Phillips, for taking what I envisioned in my mind, and exceeding all expectations on the exterior layout of the book.

To my three boys, Braxton, Jordan, and Caden for always loving me and bringing so much happiness to my life. To Tracy, my sweetheart, for standing by me, through the tough times and for believing in me, even when I made poor choices.

Finally, and most of all, to my Dad who taught me how to work hard. Without his influence on my life, I would never have been able to get to the gym at 5:00 am every day and put in 10 to 12 hours a day for twenty years. Even at 80 years old battling cancer, he never complains, and is still the hardest working man I know. I love you, Dad!

From Jen:

There is no way I would have had the time to complete this book if it wasn't for the help of my husband, Jake. He stepped up to take care of things around the house when I was lost in my laptop. Not to mention the endless dishes he washed as I experimented in the kitchen. He also became my official taste tester (though that probably ended up a plus in his book).

To my son, Jonathan, my reason for doing everything I do and my constant ray of sunshine. I already know, even at four, that you will do amazing things in your life.

To my parents, thanks for teaching me dedication. You never let me give up, always believed in me, and pushed me to do more and be better.

To my sister, Michelle, my Mom, and my Aunts for sharing their love of the kitchen with me and helping me with some of the recipes found in the book.

To Dale & Robyn Peake, Judy Malinowski, Talya Drissman, Brandon & Scott Kreft, Sarah Weingarden, my good friends, my sounding boards, leaders and mentors, you all have given me so much.

Finally, to Mike, for allowing me to work with you on the first book and agreeing to partner with me on the cookbook, back when I just though it would be something cool to do. Who knew emailing a guy from YouTube could lead to so much.

About The Authors

Mike Page graduated in 1991 from the University of Utah with a Bachelor's Degree in Exercise and Sports Science. He built the largest personal training business in Utah, at one point, employing over 60 trainers. Mike has performed over 50,000 individual personal training appointments, and has worked individually with over 4,000 clients. Three and a half years ago, Mike started working on a fast fat loss system called "The Page Cycle," that was released in November 2011. Currently, over 30,000 people in over 32 countries are utilizing Mike's program with great success. The Page Cycle is a "Food Cycling" program that enables people to see instant results, combined with a long term plan to keep the weight off forever.

Jennifer Du Charme is a busy work-from-home-mom. She graduated from Oakland University in 2008 with a Bachelors Degree in Business, a major in Human Resources Management and a minor in Communications. After a year working in her field of Human Resources, she sought a new path that would allow her the time freedom to spend with her little boy, Jonathan. Jen started working with Mike Page as the editor or the Page Cycle Diet Book and later they joined forces again to create the Cookbook. After losing weight herself on the Page Cycle Diet, she strives to empower others to take control of their lives and live it in a healthier and fuller way.

13431357R00089

Made in the USA
Charleston, SC
10 July 2012